CLOSING THE GAP

CLOSING THE GAP

SUSTAINABLE INFRASTRUCTURE
TO SAVE THE WORLD

ANDY RUAN

NEW DEGREE PRESS
COPYRIGHT © 2021 ANDY RUAN
All rights reserved.

CLOSING THE GAP
Sustainable Infrastructure to Save the World

ISBN   978-1-63676-717-8   *Paperback*
                978-1-63730-050-3   *Kindle Ebook*
                978-1-63730-152-4   *Ebook*

*FOR MY MOM, DAD, AND BROTHER,
WHO HAVE GIVEN ME EVERYTHING*

Contents

	INTRODUCTION	9
CHAPTER 1.	THE NEED FOR INFRASTRUCTURE	23
CHAPTER 2.	THE GAP	37
CHAPTER 3.	CLIMATE CHANGE	55
CHAPTER 4.	COOKING	79
CHAPTER 5.	CONFLICT	95
CHAPTER 6.	DELIVERING INFRASTRUCTURE TO THE WORLD	119
CHAPTER 7.	A PERFECT PAIRING	135
CHAPTER 8.	RISKY BUSINESS	153
CHAPTER 9.	RETHINKING THE ROLE OF GOVERNMENT	165
CHAPTER 10.	PUBLIC-PRIVATE PARTNERSHIPS	177
CHAPTER 11.	THE OPPORTUNITY OF A LIFETIME	201
CHAPTER 12.	SWING FOR THE FENCES	219
	ACKNOWLEDGMENTS	235
	APPENDIX	237

INTRODUCTION

—

If you ever find yourself driving north out of the Egyptian city of Aswan, you'll encounter a landscape typical for the nation, something you might imagine if you were asked to draw up a mental picture of Egypt. Vast stretches of arid, sunbaked desert stretching as far as the eye can see. If you can picture that, you have a decent idea of what most of Egypt looks like.

Keep driving for thirty-five kilometers, and all of that changes. You'll see a flat, dark blue line rising above the tan horizon from the left side of the road. Five more kilometers and you'll find the Benban Solar Park, one of the largest photovoltaic solar energy systems in the world, a massive grid of panels so vast it is easily visible from space.[1]

The story of renewable energy in Egypt is one that defies all expectations. Barely half a decade ago, the situation could not have been more different. Following the Arab Spring in 2012, Egypt began facing an energy crisis. The rapidly expanding

---

1   Lewis, "Giant Solar Park."

population was demanding more and more power, particularly for air-conditioning during the sweltering summer months. Meanwhile, a swiftly depreciating power grid and a decline in resource availability were causing energy supplies to dwindle. The country began its transition from an energy exporter to energy importer.[2]

Blackouts were frequent and protracted, with forced power cuts happening up to six times a day for hours on end. Public transport came to a standstill, cable networks were pulled off the air, and business production took a turn for the worse.[3]

"No electricity, no educated kids," said one mother, expressing a sentiment shared by many concerned parents at the time.[4] Children were forced to study outside at night by streetlight. Five years ago, no policymaker, academic, or development professional would have held out hope for Egypt. Few Egyptians held out hope for Egypt. In late 2014, "Have Mercy on Us" was the message displayed on the cover of al-Gomhoria, a state-owned newspaper.[5]

The energy situation across most of the developing world is just as dire as Egypt's was. In the West African nation of Mali, the average household uses less electricity in an entire year than would take to boil a kettle in London.[6] Over 770 million people lack any access to electricity altogether.[7] While

---

2   ESMAP, *Maximizing Finance*, 1.
3   Schwartzstein, "Egypt's Crisis."
4   The World Bank, "Egypt's Extra Electricity."
5   Kingsley, "Egypt Suffers Regular Blackouts."
6   Hussain et al., "Unlocking."
7   IEA, *SDG 7: Data and Projections*.

buildings in the developed world light up the night sky in a brilliant display of human ingenuity, entire countries are bathed in darkness when the sun goes down.

In the twenty-first century, as technological innovations have accelerated past humanity's wildest dreams, it isn't difficult to look past a world left behind. We live in an age where intelligent vehicles can ferry a person across hundreds of miles at the same time a third of the global population lacks access to safe drinking water and sanitation.[8] Though rapid economic growth in the last century has brought some level of prosperity to the poorest parts of the world, over 700 million people remain in extreme poverty.[9] Real and intense suffering is still widespread. To say nothing of pleasures and freedoms, extreme and growing inequalities exists at the most basic, fundamental levels of human life.

The aforementioned numbers are certainly daunting, though they come on the back of massive improvements made in recent decades. Since the 1900s, advancements in global connectivity, technology, and modern medicines have facilitated a kind of rapid economic growth and development never before seen in human history. Global average life expectancy at 72.6 years is higher than any single country's average in 1950, and billions have been lifted out of poverty.[10]

Still, this progress has yet to reach many parts of the developing world, and the people untouched by prosperity are

---

8   UNICEF/WHO, *Progress*, 49.
9   World Bank, *Reversals of Fortune*, 28.
10 Roser, Ortiz-Ospina, and Ritchie, "Life Expectancy."

becoming increasingly concentrated. Of the twenty countries with the highest poverty rates, eighteen of them are in sub-Saharan Africa. If current trends continue, sub-Saharan Africa will be home to the vast majority of the world's extreme poor in both proportion and absolute numbers by 2030. Even within the region, almost half of the poor already live in just five countries: Nigeria, the Democratic Republic of the Congo, Tanzania, Ethiopia, and Madagascar.[11]

Neither is continued progress guaranteed for the future. For the first time in over twenty years, global extreme poverty is on the rise. Our world is now facing three converging crises that are driving this reversal. The 2020 edition of the World Bank's flagship *Poverty and Shared Prosperity Report* identifies them as COVID-19, armed conflict, and climate change. These three challenges have the potential to permanently alter the future of human development.[12]

The pandemic and its resulting recession are projected to push 124 million additional people below the extreme poverty line, the greatest reversal in the decline of global poverty in the last three decades.[13] Entire industries grinded to a halt in the deepest recession since the Great Depression, and labor markets were disrupted like never before.[14] The situation has grown to such epic proportions that its ramifications will be felt for decades to come.

---

11 Schoch and Lakner, "Mixed Progress."
12 World Bank, *Reversals of Fortune*, xi.
13 Lakner et al., "Updated Estimates."
14 International Labor Organization, *Covid-19 and the World of Work*.

Even as the world struggles through the pandemic, it finds itself on the eve of another crisis, one with consequences that could be even more widespread and severe. Climate change, due to the rise in global temperatures, threatens to wreak environmental and economic havoc across the planet. The same World Bank report estimates an additional 132 million people will fall into poverty from the aggregate effects of climate change. Rising sea levels endanger entire populations living in coastal areas. Protracted droughts and heat waves will lead to reduced crop and livestock productivity, creating massive food and water insecurities. Ecological transformation will exacerbate existing insecurities and push fragile economic and political systems to their very limits.[15]

Increasingly frequent extreme weather events like hurricanes and floods have the potential to wipe out entire cities and displace millions of people. In 2007, droughts and agricultural destruction drove people from rural areas in Syria away from their homes. Researchers at the National Academy of Sciences concluded that the additional stress placed on cities helped to ignite the uprisings that turned into the Syrian Civil War.[16] Millions more were displaced as a result of violent conflict, leading to the Syrian refugee crisis. In total, over six million people have been forcibly uprooted in the war-torn nation.[17]

Terrible as they are, those numbers pale in comparison to the amount of people who could be displaced by the manifold

---

15 World Bank, *Reversals of Fortune*, 1.
16 Kelley et al., "Syrian drought."
17 Edwards, "Syrian Refugees."

effects of climate change. Researchers at The International Bank for Reconstruction and Development (IBRD) estimated in 2018 that more than 140 million people in sub-Saharan Africa, South Asia, and Latin America will have to migrate away from their home communities. For fragile and conflict-affected nations, it's a humanitarian crisis waiting to happen on a scale we've never seen before.[18]

Let me be clear. Climate change is not just another hurdle like any other that poor countries have traditionally struggled through. It is not about slowing economic growth. It isn't about any of the traditional goals a developing company might have.

It is about existence itself.

As consumed as the world is now with fending off the worst of the global pandemic, climate change is not far off into the future. Pan-African research institute Afrobarometer conducted the largest ever survey on the views of Africans on climate change between 2016 and 2018 and found 67 percent of respondents who had heard of climate change said it was making their lives worse.[19]

As Jim Yong Kim, twelfth president of the World Bank, put it in 2018, "There's not a single African leader who won't tell you that the boot of climate change is on their necks."[20]

---

18 World Bank, "Climate Change."
19 Selormey and Logan, "African Nations."
20 Kim, "Human Capital and Technology."

At the same time, another important trend is emerging: Aspirations are rising. It isn't uncommon these days to see a group of young children in rural Somalia, Ethiopia, or Bangladesh huddled around a smart phone. Their homes may be worn down and they may have to walk miles to find a safe source of drinking water, but one way or another, their access to the Internet is growing. A 2018 UN report found that four in five people in the world's least developed countries have access to a mobile-cellular network. On top of that, broadband coverage in these countries is nearing 100 percent.[21]

Access to the Internet can mean progress toward growth and development. However, it also means the poorest people in the world know exactly how everyone else lives. If you are a resident of a wealthy nation, you may have little to no idea what it's like to live in the developing world. But you certainly have the opportunity to research it. The reverse is now also true. Trust that the lifestyle you enjoy and the opportunities you pursue are fully visible. And for all of your own aspirations, know they are shared by those who do not enjoy the pre-conditions of bodily and societal wellbeing. What will happen when those aspirations are not met?

That realization was earth-shattering to me. As messed up as it is to say, the knowledge that the ridiculously excessive set of opportunities afforded to me are well-publicized to the least privileged parts of the world is almost as shocking as the inequalities themselves. The scale and implications of global inequality are no longer the realm of academics and

---

21   United Nations, "Universal and Affordable Internet."

journalists. They are fully displayed in high definition for the entire world population to contend with.

No country will remain untouched by any of the great crises, but the brunt of the pain will be felt by the poor. It is the most vulnerable among us who will be obstructed from achieving inclusive, sustainable growth. Conflict, climate change, and pandemics will converge and interact in ways not yet foreseeable. Understanding these challenges to the best of our ability and finding ways to address them are now among humanity's greatest imperatives.

Of course, each challenge possesses its own individual complexities, most of which are beyond the scope of this book or any single book you might encounter. Instead, this text focuses on a single aspect of sustainable development that will be central to the fight against all three: infrastructure.

Infrastructure underpins all economic and social activity. The quality and quantity of infrastructure is one of the key indicators of a developing country's transition into an emerging economy and eventually into a developed one. When roads, power grids, and effective ports are built, the private sector can invest in more productive, export-oriented activities, thus improving employment, human capital, and competitiveness. In times of recession, infrastructure spending can stimulate demand, provide jobs, and improve the efficiency of energy and logistics. Quality transport infrastructure can massively reduce transaction costs and enable economies of scale. Energy infrastructure is the lifeblood of any healthy economy. Water infrastructure is vital to human health. Telecommunications infrastructure is the key to the future.[22]

By extension, and through the provision of basic services, infrastructure plays a major role in reducing poverty and improving various aspects of a societal wellbeing. There is robust evidence supporting the positive influence of investments in infrastructure on poverty, health, education, environmental sustainability and social equality.[23] It isn't too difficult to see why.

Imagine waking up one day and finding your lights and air conditioning won't turn on and no running water will come out of your kitchen or bathroom appliances. You look out the window and see all the roads leading to and from your home are gone. What would you do? How would you start your day?

While even the poorest households in high-income nations benefit from vast networks of roads, power grids, water facilities, and telecommunications towers, the same cannot be said of the poorest households in developing nations. These deficits are some of the biggest impediments to achieving sustainable development. Without sufficient investment in infrastructure assets, there is little hope for low-income countries to catch up to the rest of the world. It is in this sense infrastructure becomes a moral imperative in addition to an economic one.

---

22 Bhattacharya et al., *Sustainable Infrastructure*, vi.
23 Ibid.

The relationships between infrastructure and development have been well-established for decades. The United Nations Office for Project Services (UNOPS) estimated in 2018 that infrastructure systems have the potential to influence the achievement of 92 percent of all targets set by the United Nations' Sustainable Development Goals. Now, in light of recent events, greater attention has also been placed on the role of infrastructure in mitigating and adapting to global crises. Megacities all throughout South Asia, for example, are responding to increasingly frequent extreme weather events through flood-resistant dams. Solar and wind power are becoming an increasingly attractive option to meet growing energy demand at low cost to the environment. Transport and logistics infrastructure, along with hospitals, have been recognized for their critical importance in fighting health crises like the pandemic.[24]

Assessing infrastructure in the context of these events has led to the emergence of an evolving concept known as "sustainable infrastructure." The Inter-American Development Bank uses a working definition as "infrastructure projects that are planned, designed, constructed, operated, and decommissioned in a manner to ensure economic and financial, social, environmental (including climate resilience), and institutional stability over the entire life cycle of the project." Sustainable infrastructure is an acknowledgment of the central role infrastructure must play in building a better future for our world. At the same time, it recognizes how failing to invest in infrastructure or implementing it poorly may

---

24 UNOPS, *Infrastructure Underpinning Sustainable Development*, 41.

compromise the economic and environmental viability of our planet for future generations.[25]

The Global Infrastructure Hub, a research agency established by the G20, estimated investment needs to be an average of $3.7 trillion per year just to maintain pace with economic growth.[26] Yet even as infrastructure needs continue to grow, levels of actual investment fall woefully short of what is needed. This is true in both developed and developing countries and is widely recognized as a problem known as the "Infrastructure Gap." Due to their relatively weaker economies and higher vulnerability to disasters, investment gaps are proportionally highest in developing countries. Meeting the SDGs to eliminate poverty and achieve universal access to drinking water, sanitation, and electricity will require even further investment, as will adaptations to climate change, violent conflict, and pandemics. Other estimates using broader definitions of infrastructure and incorporating requirements toward meeting the Sustainable Development Goals reveal even higher needs, around five-to-six trillion dollars per year. Current investment levels, according the World Bank and the OECD, trail these needs by up to three trillion dollars per year.[27]

A number of persisting reasons inhibit countries from closing their infrastructure gaps. Governments in developing countries find themselves suffocated by debt, unable to find the fiscal space to spend more on infrastructure. Weak institutions

---

25 IADB, *What is Sustainable Infrastructure*, 3.
26 Global Infrastructure Hub, *Global Infrastructure Outlook*, 24.
27 OECD/The World Bank/ UN Environment, *Financing Climate Futures*, 20.

and a general lack of capacity prevent the kind of robust planning necessary to implement projects. Corruption and instability jeopardize planning, transaction and construction stages. International donors fail to cooperate on sustainable infrastructure projects and provide the level of assistance developing countries need.[28]

Closing the infrastructure gap isn't impossible. Egypt, despite being located in the heart of the climate crisis and experiencing its worst energy situation in recent history, managed to turn the situation around and build one of the largest, most successful solar parks on the planet. Through the right combination of financing techniques, good governance, and technical expertise, Egypt was able to achieve a 360-degree reversal of an energy crisis many believed to be intractable.[29]

But success stories like Egypt's, along with a handful of others, are few and far between. Too many barriers exist to replicate those projects in all the countries that need them. Closing the infrastructure gap will be exceedingly difficult, but it cannot be ignored. The implications would be devastating. Tackling this colossal challenge will require the combined effort of multiple generations of courageous policymakers, investors, academics, development professionals, and everyday citizens. By taking advantage of emerging technologies and innovative financial mechanisms, we can go farther towards closing the infrastructure gap than ever before.

---

28   Bhattacharya et al., *Sustainable Infrastructure*.
29   ESMAP, *Maximizing Finance*.

This book is merely a small part of that great effort. In it, you will read about the challenges and crises facing many parts of the developing world. You will discover the exact role infrastructure might play in fighting global crises, stimulating growth, and spreading shared prosperity across the planet. You will find lessons gleaned from infrastructure projects built in the unlikeliest of places and financed by the most unprecedented kinds of investors, and you will learn about the kinds of win-win solutions that can usher in a brighter future for us all. And, I hope, perhaps you will find a newfound passion for infrastructure and for tackling the great challenges of our time.

The chapters are organized as follows. Chapter One provides an overview of infrastructure and its historical role in growth and development. Chapter Two introduces the global infrastructure gap and its main drivers. Chapters Three through Five detail specific development challenges related to global crises of conflict and climate change. Chapters Six through Eight explore infrastructure as a financial asset and barriers to private involvement in infrastructure. Chapters Nine and Ten detail case studies and stories of successful investments in emerging markets infrastructure. Chapter Eleven discusses the effects of the COVID-19 pandemic on development and the imperative to build resilience and sustainability in its wake. Finally, Chapter Twelve concludes with a personal narrative about my journey in discovering the infrastructure gap and finding my voice to talk about it. I hope you will find these chapters interesting, challenging, and worthwhile.

1

THE NEED FOR INFRASTRUCTURE

At the beginning of the COVID-19 pandemic, I was living in a small one-bedroom apartment in Nashville, Tennessee. The building wasn't the newest. The floors were covered in rough, worn carpet, and the walls were painted a sickly shade of yellow. Most of my tables and chairs were the foldable kind people leave out by the dumpsters after they move out. The wood underlying the countertops of the kitchen sink had been rotting since I moved in, and a handful of splinters would crumble onto the floor each time I opened a cabinet. By many standards, I lived relatively modestly. But I loved that apartment. It was situated high enough in the building to give me a view of the city's rising skyscrapers and burgeoning downtown district. I lived close enough to the buildings I worked and studied in, and I had all the amenities I needed. I was happy to call it my home.

While I was living there, I had a very regular morning routine. Upon waking, I would roll off the left side of my mattress and walk straight into the bathroom. I'd turn on the tap, letting the flowing water remove the sleep from my eyes. Most days, I would hop into the shower for a quick rinse. After washing up, I'd roll up the blinds and slide open one of my windows facing downtown. From the day I moved in, there had been a faint musty odor that, for the life of me, I could not identify the origin of. Letting in a bit of fresh air always helped.

After my bathroom routine, I would fill up a filtered pitcher with water at the kitchen sink, probably while maneuvering around a pile of unwashed dishes I left from the previous night. With a glass of water, I would settle down behind the laptop on my desk, where it sat charging through the night.

Riveting stuff, right? Why did I just describe such a mundane set of tasks? There certainly isn't anything special about my morning routine. You might do something very similar every day.

Consider the average young woman from Kafle, a small village in the north of Ethiopia. Like me, a normal morning routine for her begins with water. Instead of using a bathroom sink just a few steps away, she walks several miles to the nearest river. If she's the oldest child in her family, the responsibility to fetch the day's worth of water has fallen on her shoulders. She straps an old jerrycan—the kind used by soldiers in the second world war—to her back and embarks on her journey. Kafle sits on top of a steep hill and the descent to the valley floor where the river flows can be dangerous.

The narrow path down hugs the side of the earth mound and the rocks are loose enough to slip out from underneath her.[30]

The nearest river is only thirty minutes away. I say "only" because the equivalent journey for many women across sub-Saharan Africa can be a whole day's affair. The scorching ninety-degree weather and the 7,000-foot elevation bear down on travelers as they traverse the land. Their destination is a shallow stream of muddy water barely deep enough to dip a cup into. Women take turns scooping as much liquid as they can get, often competing with cows and goats for the few spots along the river where water flows unencumbered. During the hot summer months, the stream is barely a trickle. Sometimes, it isn't there at all. On a good day, after a great deal of scooping, one can fill an entire five-gallon jerrycan full of water. Carrying the additional forty pounds, the young women make the long trek back up the hill to their village.[31]

In the half hour it takes me to go through my morning routine, I will have consumed roughly twenty gallons of clean water, five times the amount an entire family uses for a whole day in Africa. This is the kind of inequality that remains prevalent in our time.[32]

POVERTY IS STILL WITH US

Despite the situation described above, there are many who now consider such conditions a thing of the past—left behind

---

30   *Charity Water*, "Life Without Clean Water."
31   Ibid.
32   Weil, "Water Use."

in premodern societies decades ago. Indeed, by many standards, the world has gotten much healthier and wealthier. Max Roser, economist at the University of Oxford, is famously quoted as saying, "On every day in the last twenty-five years, there could have been a newspaper headline reading, 'The number of people in extreme poverty fell by 128,000 since yesterday.'"[33] At least before the COVID-19 pandemic, his statement was completely accurate. Extreme poverty declined from 36 percent of the global population in 1990 to below 10 percent in 2015. Given these developments, a positive outlook on the current state of the world's poor might be expected.[34]

Over the same period, access to basic infrastructure services was also growing at unprecedented rates. The number of people without access to electricity dropped to around 770 million in 2019, a record low. As access was already near-universal in the developed world, this increase was largely driven by progress in low and middle-income countries. Since 1990, almost 1.2 billion people gained access to electricity in developing Asia. In 2019, the government of India declared it had reached over 99 percent electricity penetration. Even in Africa, countries like Kenya were able to raise access rates to 85 percent from below 20 percent a decade before.[35]

Access to improved water sources, defined by the WHO as a "piped household water connection located inside the user's

---

33 Roser and Ortiz-Ospina, "Global Extreme Poverty."
34 World Bank, "Decline of Global Extreme Poverty."
35 IEA, *SDG7*.

dwelling, plot, or yard" has followed a similar trajectory.[36] In 1990, over 1.2 billion people did not have such access. By 2015, that number was cut in half, and most countries had water-access rates above 90 percent. Over the twenty-five-year period, an additional 107 million people gained access to an improved water source every year.[37]

These trends are certainly worth acknowledging. By many accounts, the world is doing better than it ever has, and one might question the necessity of a book about poverty and infrastructure in developing countries. If the year 2020 can be written off as an anomaly, should not the world simply do the best it can to return to its original path and stay on par for the course?

Far from it.

A closer examination of the metrics used to measure both extreme poverty and access to infrastructure paints a different picture. Improvements have been unevenly distributed, and the lion's share of progress has been limited to a select group of countries. China itself has lifted more than 850 million people above the International Poverty Line since 1981, representing over three-quarters of the entire world's progress during that time.[38]

Growth in access to infrastructure services has been similarly unequal. Two-thirds of the improvements in electricity

---

36   WHO/UNICEF Joint Monitoring Programme for Water Supply and Sanitation, *Progress*, 22.
37   Ritchie, "Clean Water."
38   Marques, "China Scores."

access are attributable to India. In Africa, just five countries are responsible for nearly all of the continent's advancements in energy: Kenya, Senegal, Rwanda, Ghana, and Ethiopia. Concentrated progress has been matched by concentrated stagnation and decline. Three-quarters of the world population without electricity now live in sub-Saharan Africa. If current trends continue, the gap between these areas and the rest of the world will only widen.[39]

With regards to water, though data has shown an increase in access to basic water and sanitation, there remain stark inequalities in the quality and availability of these services. According to UNICEF and the WHO, 2.2 billion people still do not have safely managed drinking water services and 4.2 billion people lack safely managed sanitation services. The deficits illustrate that mere access is not enough. Water, sanitation, and hygiene services are still too unsafe or located too far away for most of the world's population.[40]

For years, development experts have debated whether the standard measure of extreme poverty is at all meaningful. The widely used International Poverty Line classifies an individual as being in extreme poverty if their level of income is below US $1.90 a day.[41] The value represents the mean of the national poverty lines found in the fifteen poorest countries in the world in terms of per capita consumption. Many suggest this standard is far too low to serve as the global benchmark. Anthropologist Jason Hickel argues a minimum daily

---

39 IEA, *SDG7*.
40 UNICEF/UN, *Progress on Household*, 8-10.
41 World Bank, "Global Poverty Line Update."

income of $7.40 per day is a necessary baseline in this day and age, regardless of the country you reside in. Incidentally, this number is much closer to the national poverty lines in many of the world's poorest countries.[42]

About a quarter of the global population lives under $3.20 USD per day and close to half lives under $5.50 USD a day. These numbers represent poverty lines commonly used for lower-middle-income and upper-middle-income countries, respectively. The reduction in poverty against these lines has been much slower than against the extreme poverty line of $1.90, suggesting hundreds of millions of people have barely escaped the lowest threshold. In fact, the total number of people below the $5.50 line has barely changed in the past thirty years, an indication of the scale of the problem that remains. Unlike the extreme poor in regions like Sub-Saharan Africa, the majority of the poor at these lines live in densely populated Asian countries. Though many have climbed out of the poorest category, their living conditions are undoubtedly still shaped by poverty and all of its hardships. For them, falling back under the extreme poverty line is an ever-present threat.[43]

These statistics reveal the fragility of the progress that has been achieved. Look no further than the COVID-19 pandemic, which, sadly, cannot be treated as a mere anomaly, because its effects will ripple long into the future. The cost to human life has been immense. Hundreds of millions have lost their livelihoods in the recession and are now teetering

---
42 Hickel, "International Poverty Line."
43 Schoch, Lakner, and Rodriguez, "Monitoring Poverty."

on the edge of extreme poverty. The sheer size of this backslide calls into question whether or not true progress was ever achieved at all.

Though many of the world's wealthy and middle-class have also suffered greatly at the hands of the pandemic, there is no question the world's poor have suffered the most. Those who had the least also had the most to lose. While others may struggle to find new job opportunities or keep their businesses open, the poor find themselves without access to food, water, shelter, heating, and other bare necessities of life. Even as countries slowly exit the pandemic, many find themselves increasingly affected by extreme weather events, resource insecurity, and other consequences imposed by climate change. Many of these nations are also struggling through or have recently exited protracted bouts of violent conflict. From 2015 to 2018, extreme poverty rates in the Middle East and North Africa nearly doubled due to conflicts in the Syrian Arab Republic and the Republic of Yemen.[44]

How can we boast of progress when so many millions of people can be thrown back into the clutches of extreme poverty at a moment's notice? Despite unprecedented advances in wealth and technology, entire nations continue to struggle to provide the bare minimum for their poorest. It is this population, already the most familiar with hardship, that will shoulder the greatest burdens imposed by conflict, climate change, and pandemics. Though the privileged seem to constantly remind us otherwise, we now have a greater pool

---

44 World Bank, *Reversals of Fortune*, 1.

of financial resources than ever before, but not enough of it is being put to use solving the three aforementioned challenges.

That the developing world and its future should be so characterized by fragility and vulnerability begs the question of what kinds of progress are most worth pursuing. Clearly, income and consumption alone, even at higher levels, are insufficient measures of the difficulties facing the world's poor. They offer little indication of individuals' preparedness to maintain their livelihoods through shocks and disasters. What then, is the right approach to promoting the opposite of fragility and vulnerability: resilience and sustainability?

INFRASTRUCTURE AS AN EVALUATIVE CRITERION
The following hypothetical example is adapted from a 2018 World Bank Report titled "Beyond Monetary Poverty."[45]

Imagine two households have the same income of five US dollars per person per day. The first household has access to safe and reliable water, sanitation, and energy services. The location of their home is also connected to several roads that afford them easy access to nearby stores and the local school. The second household is situated in an area without the necessary infrastructure to provide such basic services. There is neither piped water nor a power grid and the nearest all-weather road is several miles away.

Of course, this second family must also drink and use some amount of water for sanitation. But instead of receiving it

---
45   World Bank, *Poverty Puzzle*, 88.

directly, they must travel hours to retrieve water by hand from the nearest well or primary source. If they're lucky, a water tanker truck may stop by their home every few days, though prices are usually prohibitively high. For sanitation, they may use an outdoor latrine with no sewage connection. Likewise, the family must also consume energy of some sort for lighting and cooking. In place of gas or electric stoves, they use traditional stoves powered by heavily polluting fuels like coal, dung, or crop waste.

Though the two households generate the same amount of income, it is clear their standards of living are very different. The welfare disparity comes from the access the first household has to infrastructure services, something not entirely captured by measures of income or consumption. Infrastructure is also what makes the first family more resilient and less vulnerable to shocks. If both households experience a loss in income, it is the second household that will be forced to spend relatively more time and effort meeting water and energy needs. The first household maintains its access to basic services and can devote more of its resources toward adapting to the crisis and purchasing other necessary goods. In other words, well-functioning infrastructure systems can provide a baseline for populations that mere income cannot.

A RESPONSE TO POVERTY AND CRISIS

Kannan Lakmeeharan is someone who witnessed the difference infrastructure can make firsthand. While studying to become an electrical engineer in college at the University of Witwatersrand in Johannesburg, Kannan spent a few weeks in rural areas of South Africa working on an electrification design project. The goal was to find ways to improve the cost effectiveness of connecting those living on the outskirts of larger cities to the energy grid. In the process of doing so, Kannan went around speaking to local residents, asking them how and why they valued electricity. From their answers, he saw the true nature of his work.

"It was about addressing the root causes preventing Africa from taking its rightful place," he shared with me.

Kannan went on to join Eskom, the largest electric public utility in South Africa. One day, he received a phone call from a friend who expressed to him some of the difficulties he was having getting connected to electricity and the struggles his family was experiencing as a result. He knew Kannan worked at Eskom and had hoped to find some help. Kannan didn't think twice. He made a couple of phone calls and ensured his friend's connection could be secured. That was routine for Kannan. It was part of the job.

"It wasn't a favor. It was the right thing to do," he said, knowing full well from his earlier years the impact energy would make.

A few weeks later, Kannan received an email from that same friend, explaining exactly how and why the electricity connection made such a difference to him and his family. He lived in a small village in the Northwest province, where energy access was especially scarce. The electricity afforded him heat, light, and enabled his children to study and do homework when the sun went down. It ended some of the most potent struggles his family was facing.

"He said the quality of his life immediately improved. I never received a letter directly from somebody thanking me, so I think that just touched me," said Kannan.

The vulnerability Kannan's friend experienced can be measured in part by the World Bank's multidimensional poverty indicator, a metric developed in recent years combining income with measures of access to basic infrastructure services. Using this standard, the global extreme poverty rate is 50 percent higher than when using the $1.90 international poverty line.[46]

Beyond ensuring individuals have access to essential resources, high-quality infrastructure assets can enable a country as a whole to fight back against crisis and recession. During the coronavirus pandemic, countries with robust systems of transport and logistics were able respond much faster and more effectively. Countries without such infrastructure had greater difficulty building supply chains for test kits, vaccines, and protective medical equipment.[47]

As Vice President and Treasurer of the World Bank, Jingdong Hua, stated in July of 2020, "The pandemic highlighted even more the critical disparity in preparedness, from health care systems to digital bandwidth to continued education for people in lockdown to remote networks that are essential for e-commerce and logistics to work."[48]

---

46 Ibid.
47 Hua, "Green Transition."
48 Ibid.

With regard to climate change, infrastructure acts as a direct response to natural resource deprivation by improving the reliability and efficiency of service provision. Water-treatment centers and desalination plants can bring clean, potable water to places affected by droughts and heatwaves. Wind and solar power can be a cheaper and more sustainable replacement for carbon-emitting fossil fuels. These assets help scale back greenhouse emissions while simultaneously bringing energy to climate-affected communities.[49]

The effects of natural disasters and extreme weather events can be tempered and even prevented by climate-resistant infrastructure. Dams and seawalls can stop rising sea levels and flood damage. Infrastructure can also ensure the sustainability of natural ecosystems. Drainage systems can help preserve water reservoirs and wetlands. Altogether, these types of infrastructure drastically reduce the vulnerability of people and ecosystems to environmental shocks.[50]

Resource scarcity is often tied to violence and conflict in places with weak governance and chronic social tensions. Such was the case with water in the Sudanese Civil War as well as with the ongoing conflicts in Israel-Palestine and Darfur.[51] As climate change continues to threaten food and water systems, such clashes are destined to grow in frequency and duration. Infrastructure and its effect on resource provision can be an important part of peacebuilding and reducing inequality in conflict-affected states. In South Sudan's Lakes

---

49 OECD, *Climate-resilient Infrastructure*
50 Ibid.
51 Amnesty International, "The Occupation of Water."

State, water reservoirs and boreholes were constructed to increase access to drinkable water. In addition to supporting immediate needs, the projects encouraged greater security and rule of law and provided economic opportunities for local communities.[52]

It is for these reasons that infrastructure is chosen here as the evaluative criterion for the path moving forward. As you read further, you will encounter a number of case examples illustrating in greater detail the profound effect infrastructure can have on building resilience and sustainability. This is not to say other aspects of development are unimportant. Certainly, greater attention to health, education, political stability, and trade policy will also be quintessential to building a better future for the poor, but infrastructure remains woefully underfunded and under-discussed despite being one of the most viable means of investing in the developing world.

---

52 Fantini and Morgan, "Conflict, Climate Change, and Infrastructure."

2

THE GAP

WHAT IS INFRASTRUCTURE?
Prior to his inauguration, President Donald Trump pledged to "build the greatest infrastructure on planet earth."[53] It was a vague and insubstantial promise at best, though the president certainly wasn't the first to make it. Infrastructure is one of those words loosely thrown around by politicians to garner support for their broader platforms. Policymakers and voters from across the political spectrum tend to agree that infrastructure generally is good, so most candidates will roll out infrastructure plans as part of their campaign platforms, usually without specifying what types of structures or services they are referring to. All of the leading contenders for the 2020 Democratic presidential did so, as did (at the time) Vice President Biden, who revealed his plan along with a scathing tweet that claimed Trump's administration "failed to deliver results."[54] Time will tell whether the Biden Administration will do much different.

---

53 Zanona, "Trump."
54 Biden, "President Trump."

What exactly is meant by the term, "infrastructure"? There isn't a universally agreed upon definition. It's a modern word that comes from the Latin prefix "infra," meaning "below," and the French word for "structure." It was first used in 1875 to describe underground construction projects like tunnels and water systems built in France. In the mid-twentieth century, the term was more commonly used to describe airfields, military bases, and transport systems built to support the war effort in various countries. By the 1970s, the term adopted more of a civilian character, referring to the systems that governments, urban planners, and civil engineers were building to improve societal living conditions.[55]

The varied uses of the word across time speak to one of its key characteristics. Infrastructure addresses societal needs, and needs are constantly evolving. In this sense, we can solve for modern variations of the definition by first identifying the foremost needs of society, then categorizing the types of physical systems and structures needed to support those needs under the broad bucket of "infrastructure."

For the purposes of both simplicity and consistency with broader academic consensus, the core infrastructure needs of any country are identified as belonging to one of these four categories: energy, water, transport, and telecom. Throughout this book, I will refer to infrastructure as the public-serving assets or systems in these sectors. The case studies in later chapters will not cover all of the following listed examples in detail. Instead, the focus will be on those assets most needed in the developing world.

---

55   Walker, "Digging."

ENERGY
- Generation: power plants, including traditional fossil fuels and renewables like solar, wind, geothermal, nuclear, biofuels, and hydroelectric
- Transmission: electrical substations, transmission lines
- Distribution: distribution substations, primary and secondary distribution lines, oil and gas pipelines
- Storage: hydroelectric dams
- Off-grid: photovoltaic solar panels, micro hydro, wind turbines, hybrid energy systems

WATER
- Collection: drainage basins, aqueducts, covered tunnels, dams, weirs, stormwater management systems
- Purification: water treatment plants, desalination plants, sewage treatment facilities, septic tanks, drain fields
- Storage: reservoirs, water tanks, water towers, cisterns, pressure vessels
- Distribution: pumping stations, pipe networks
- Reuse: sewage and wastewater collection systems

TRANSPORT
- Roads, railways, and highways
- Trucking terminals
- Canals and waterways
- Airports and airways
- Sea ports and container terminals
- Refueling depots

TELECOM
- Communication towers
- Optical fiber installation

- Cell towers
- Radio antennae
- Data networks
- Telephone wires

Two final considerations will help round out our definition. First, infrastructure must provide some sort of public service or promote some public goal. This is not the same as being publicly owned. No matter who the asset belongs to, so long as the service it provides is broadly available to the public, we will classify it as infrastructure. In other words, the specific actors involved in the life cycle of the infrastructure asset are less relevant than the asset itself. Government agencies, private companies, institutional investors, development finance institutions, and NGOs can each play a number of roles with regard to the planning, financing, construction, and operation of infrastructure.

Second, though the effects of infrastructure may well be abstract and intangible, the infrastructure itself must be some physical, tangible asset. Thus, something like the well-functioning of government institutions would not qualify, though elsewhere it may be loosely referred to as part of the "infrastructure" of society.

MIRACLES OF GROWTH
In the second half of the twentieth century, several countries in East Asia began to grow seriously fast. Hong Kong, Taiwan, Korea, and Singapore, together known as the "Four Asian Tigers," each maintained exceptionally high GDP growth rates from the early 1960s to the 1990s. Japan and China had

a similar, if not even more impressive trajectory. Before then, these regions were amongst the poorest and most underdeveloped countries in the world. Japan, the richest economy in East Asia at the time, had a GDP per capita level with South Africa and Chile. Korea, the poorest in the region, had a GDP per capita less than half of those of Honduras and Ghana.[56]

The transformation of Korea after the Korean War became commonly referred to as "The Miracle on the Han River."[57] And no wonder, because the amount of poverty reduction that took place was nothing short of miraculous. The percentage of people in Asia below the extreme poverty line of $1.90 fell from 48.5 percent to just 2.6 percent in 2014. That, along with record improvements in infant mortality, life expectancy, and education levels, was truly spectacular. Without the progress made in Asia, the world would never have achieved the United Nation's Millennium Development Goal of halving extreme poverty by 2015.[58]

A number of theories have originated over the years about the source of this rapid growth. In a 1993 report titled "The East Asian Miracle," the World Bank credited "market friendly" strategies like export-oriented trade policy, deregulation, and privatization.[59] As it turned out, with the exception of Hong Kong, the East Asian development experience wasn't so much driven by neoliberalism as it was by state intervention and

---

56 Chang, *East Asian Development Experience*, 1.
57 KOREA.net, "Miracle on the Hangang River."
58 WIDER, UNU, *Snapshot of Poverty*.
59 IADB, *The East Asian Mircale*, vi.

activist strategies backed by large public enterprise sectors and macroeconomic policy that incentivized investment.[60]

Still, given their extraordinary success and the diverse range of development frameworks employed, the East Asian economies have long been the subject of academic and policy disputes. One undeniable commonality between these countries, however, was their heavy emphasis on investment in one particular sector: infrastructure. Infrastructure investment in the growing East Asian countries massively outpaced emerging economies in other parts of the world. China invested up to 9 percent of its GDP into infrastructure in the 1990s and 2000s.[61] Thailand and Vietnam have investment rates exceeding 7 percent, with the rest of the region investing around 5 percent.[62]

By allocating greater savings to infrastructure sectors, particularly in roads and ports, these countries were able to rapidly scale up the productivity and efficiency of their industrial and manufacturing sectors. Businesses and individuals had greater access to new markets and economic opportunities, which, combined with investment in education, rapidly drove up human capital. In contrast, other developing regions like Latin America and Africa invested closer to 2 percent of their GDP in infrastructure. This was partly a result of the United States and the IMF advising governments of these countries to cut their spending to avoid unsustainable levels of debt and inflation. These economies have suffered from a number of

---

60 Chang, *East Asian Development Experience*, 2.
61 Bazi and Firzli, "Age of Austerity."
62 Commission on Growth and Development, *Strategies for Sustained Growth*, 35.

developmental bottlenecks as a result of inadequate transportation networks and aging power grids.[63]

The lesson learned from the East Asian countries gave rise to another lens with which to view underdevelopment: the infrastructure gap. These countries proved how critical infrastructure was to both generating and supporting growth. According to the McKinsey Global Institute, infrastructure investment has a "socioeconomic return rate" of 20 percent, meaning each additional dollar of infrastructure spending can boost GDP by twenty cents in the long run. As countries get bigger and richer, the demand for infrastructure increases even further. Businesses need power and water to expand their production and more transportation is needed to move people and goods. Development challenges related to poverty, water, and energy access are also closely related to the quantity and quality of infrastructure.[64]

POPULATION GROWTH

Much work has been done assessing global infrastructure needs compared to current levels of spending. Data in this area is still lacking due to inconsistent definitions and differences in how countries record fiscal expenditures. Unpredictability regarding climate change and levels of future growth makes assessing needs an even more uncertain task. Unfortunately, one thing has been made very clear: The majority of the world is facing severe underinvestment in infrastructure. Not surprisingly, developing countries, which have

---

63 Bhattacharya et al., *Sustainable Infrastructure*, 21.
64 Garemo, Hjerpe, and Halleman, *A Better Road*, 5.

more room to grow relative to advanced economies, have the largest deficits.

Several drivers have been expanding the global need for infrastructure independent of the three great challenges, namely population growth and urbanization. The rise in global population and the increased concentration of people in dense urban environments pose significant challenges of their own. Most of this is occurring in Africa, where fertility rates are comparatively higher than the rest of the world. In 2015, the average woman in Africa had 4.7 children, compared to the global average of 2.5. Growing at around 2.7 percent, twice as fast as Latin America or South Asia, the total population of Africa could double by 2050. That would be the equivalent of adding the entire population of Thailand every two years. In three decades, a quarter of all the people in the world will be in Africa.[65]

The long-term sustainability of population growth has been called into question for centuries. In 1978, British Economist Thomas Malthus famously published *An Essay on the Principle of Population*, in which he essentially argued that populations grow at a faster rate than food supply and all people would eventually end up starving and impoverished.[66] His theories were largely disproved when technology evolved beyond subsistence levels of agriculture, but the relationship between population growth and its own sustainability has been investigated ever since.

---

65 *The Economist*, "Africa's Population."
66 Malthus, *An Essay*.

The modern-day challenge lies in the fact that population growth is increasingly paired with a lack of development and ecological destruction. Fast-growing countries tend to be poorer, and women tend to have lower status and fewer opportunities. All else equal, population growth is associated with higher consumption, which puts greater pressure on natural resources like water and fertile land.

The problem is indicative of how messed up the world's relationship to the environment has become. Rich countries in the global North have largely gotten away with exploiting the natural environment. Their accumulation of wealth and transition to developed status has been accompanied by a significant reduction in fertility rates. The global North also creates the majority of environmental pressures because of its relatively higher carbon footprint. Meanwhile, poor countries in the global South are forced to deal with these pressures, despite contributing far less to global emissions. As populations continues to grow, the resource-depleting effects of drought, soil degradation, and desertification will become more and more potent.[67]

Addressing high population growth naturally involves efforts to lower fertility rates. Of particular importance is the social and economic empowerment of women. Access to education for females has a significant negative effect on childbearing. Schooling increases literacy rates and awareness of family planning resources. It can empower women to make their own reproductive choices. Educated women have more opportunities to pursue intellectually stimulating careers

---

67 UN Environment, *Global Environment Outlook*, 25.

and can take on more productive responsibilities inside companies and governance institutions. In Africa, women without formal education have six children on average, compared to four and two for women who complete primary and secondary schooling, respectively.[68]

Education not only reduces the total number of children women have, but it also helps to delay the timing of childbearing. One of the biggest drivers of high population growth is the young age at which women first become mothers. This increases the length of time women have to bear children. Younger mothers have less opportunity to complete their educations and negotiate their role in childrearing. Shortening the gap between each successive generation has a multiplicative effect on population growth and decreases the average age of the population. This is particularly relevant in Africa, where the average age is now just nineteen years old, compared to twenty-nine in India and thirty-seven in China.[69]

Though such trends can be tempered by changes in policy and behavior, the consensus amongst global estimates is that aggregate population will continue to grow. In Africa, so many women are of child-bearing age that even if all of them decided today to have fewer children, the population would still grow. According to the 2019 version of the United Nations *Global Environmental Outlook*, "four trends can be predicted with confidence: the world population will continue to grow, average age will increase, populations will

---

68 *The Economist*, "Africa's Population."
69 Hajjar, "The Children's Continent."

become more urban, and household sizes will become smaller."[70]

If population growth is inevitable, so too are its associated development challenges. Higher population leads to greater demand for basic infrastructure services like clean water, energy, and transportation. Given that assets are already insufficient in most of the developing world, population growth will only exacerbate the strain on aging power grids and leaking water mains.

Several emerging economies have been transitioning from being primarily agrarian to focusing on more productive sectors like manufacturing. Globalized trade has also become a critical part of countries' development. Businesses that seek to participate in this new economy need reliable energy to support their production as well as quality networks of roads, railways, and ports for shipping, logistics, and supply chain development. For many countries, this structural shift will be critical to unlocking economic growth and bringing greater prosperity to long-impoverished rural populations.[71]

Beyond simply meeting demand, sustainable infrastructure also has the potential to make consumption and production patterns more efficient and less damaging to the environment. Almost by nature, public infrastructure assets promote collective use and broad public externalities. Public transport and roads drastically reduce the cost of resource provision. Renewable energy can decouple production processes from

---

70 UN Environment, *Global Environment Outlook*, 28.
71 Bhattacharya et al., *Sustainable Infrastructure*, 22-23.

carbon emissions, making industrial and manufacturing sectors more sustainable and less damaging to the environment. With the right infrastructure, countries can meet the needs of populations while maintaining economic growth.

URBANIZATION

In addition to fast population growth, developing countries are increasingly faced with another demographic shift: urbanization. Urbanization has historically been an important part of a country's development trajectory. Cities have higher rates of economic growth and technological innovation. They offer a higher density of education and infrastructure services. People move to cities in search of better economic opportunities and higher income. Urbanization can thus be an important source of wealth creation and poverty alleviation.

On the flip side, urbanization can also be a driver of inequality, social exclusion, environmental degradation, and disease. When large amounts of people congregate in small spaces, the poor and marginalized tend to find themselves on the fringes of society, separated from the opportunities and wealth of the center. Access to quality education, clean water, and health care can become unequally distributed. The effects of air pollution, waste disposal, and sewage runoff are often dumped on the poor, rendering their neighborhoods dirty and unlivable. Combined with congestion and a lack of sanitation services, these areas can quickly become breeding grounds for communicable diseases and other health hazards.[72]

Poor neighborhoods are also more likely to be placed in geographically precarious areas like riverbanks and hillsides, making them more vulnerable to flooding, landslides, and industrial hazards. With people practically living on top of each other, the destructive potential of natural disasters grows exponentially. All of these conditions lend themselves to higher rates of crime and social unrest. Poor urban women are especially at risk.[73]

Like population growth, urbanization is largely inevitable. For the first time in history, more people live in urban instead of rural areas, and even more people are migrating to dense cities and towns. Just above half of the world's population currently lives in urban areas. According to the United Nations, that proportion will rise to 60 percent by 2030 and 66.4 percent by 2050. In fact, global population growth will be driven almost exclusively by these places, and almost all of it will take place in low-income nations. Africa is not only the fastest growing region in terms of total population, but it's also the most rapidly urbanizing.[74]

The slum-like conditions described above are already endured by a third of global urban population. Whether or not slums continue to grow in quantity and size depends on the degree to which urbanization can be planned and regulated. At the

---

72 UN Environment, *Global Environment Outlook*, 31-33.
73 Kuddus, Tynan, McBryde, "Urbanization."
74 United Nations, "Expanding Opportunities."

very heart of this challenge is infrastructure. With greater investments in sustainable infrastructure, cities can become more inclusive in their provision of basic services and more protective of the environment. The future of urbanization might very well lend itself to sustainability and prosperity. However, if current trends are allowed to continue, the social, economic, and environmental costs will be dire. Consider the following passage from the *Global Environmental Outlook*:

"If new cities are built over the next two or three decades on a resource-hungry, carbon-intensive model, based on sprawling urbanization, all hope of meeting ambitious resource and climate-risk targets will be lost. This could leave cities and countries struggling to meet their resource needs and unable to compete in global markets, with the stranding of physical and human assets. Cities are also vulnerable to environmental and climate impacts such as heat, water stress, and floods; while coastal cities face sea level rise, saltwater incursion and storm surges."[75]

Fortunately, none of these risks are inherent to urbanization. Effective institutional planning with a focus on sustainable infrastructure can change the future of urban development and decouple its negative effects on the environment. With the right policies, countries can take advantage of larger populations congregating in smaller spaces and minimize their ecological footprint. Energy is of particular importance, given its indispensable role as an engine of economic growth. Solar and wind resources can be drawn on without depletion, but consumption of these resources is limited by the stock of

---

75 UN Environment, *Global Environment Outlook*, 34-35.

physical infrastructure. Land and water use can also be more efficiently and equitably distributed through infrastructure. Governments will have to take care to monitor the inclusiveness of infrastructure services. This means taking social justice into serious consideration to make sure the poor are not left behind.

THE INFRASTRUCTURE GAP

Given the inevitability of population growth and urbanization, it's clear the world's need for infrastructure is greater than ever. The McKinsey Global Institute estimated in 2017 that the world needs to raise its infrastructure investment up to $3.7 trillion every year through 2035, *just to keep pace with economic growth*.[76] Compared to projected levels of spending, this represents a deficit of $350 billion per year. A joint report by Oxford Economics and the Global Infrastructure Hub (GIH) in 2017 also estimated investment needs to be an average of $3.7 trillion per year. This study, however, predicts an annual deficit of around $500 billion per year.[77]

Taking into account higher demand for infrastructure in recent years, Bhattacharya et al. estimate baseline investment needs to be even higher. Using growth assumptions and assessments of national investment plans to project required rates, they estimate the annual need to be around five trillion dollars, implying an even greater gap.[78] Like historical spending, the exact size of the gap varies by region.

---

76 Woetzel, *Bridging Infrastructure*, 2.
77 Global Infrastructure Hub, *Global Infrastructure Outlook*, 24.
78 Bhattacharya et al., *Sustainable Infrastructure*, vii.

For instance, according to the GIH study, Asia will have the largest overall need for infrastructure, due to its large and dense populations but is predicted to have a relatively small investment gap. Africa and Latin America, in contrast, are forecasted to have much wider gaps, at 47 percent and 39 percent, respectively. Again, these amounts are only what is required to support projected economic growth—that is to say, independent of any other objectives, the world is already facing massive infrastructure deficits.[79]

But infrastructure is not just important for economic growth. It's needed for solving real development challenges and building resilience and sustainability in vulnerable countries. That means investing even more into infrastructure specifically targeted at basic service provision and improving the lives of the poor. According to the McKinsey study, meeting the UN's Sustainable Development Goals, namely universal access to water, sanitation, and electricity, would triple the size of the estimated $350 billion deficit. That makes the true relevant size of the infrastructure gap well over one trillion dollars.[80]

Each of the aforementioned studies, however, was conducted before the start of the COVID-19 pandemic. The long-term effects of climate change and violent conflict were also largely excluded. There are several reasons why these challenges cannot be ignored. As the current global health crisis has illustrated, disastrous events can impose major setbacks to both economic growth and development. The ability of

---

79 Global Infrastructure Hub, *Global Infrastructure Outlook*, 4.
80 Woetzel, *Bridging Infrastructure Gaps*, 7-8.

countries to respond to these challenges at a systematic level is heavily dependent on their infrastructure. Whether it be a fast-spreading virus or an extreme weather event, infrastructure can help soften the blow. It allows the poor to protect access to basic services while maintaining economic resilience for the country as a whole.

With regards to climate change specifically, a transformation of infrastructure will be necessary not only to mitigate negative effects, but also to build a pathway to minimize carbon emissions and limit global temperature increases to below two degrees Celsius. Currently, meeting the world's energy, transport, and water needs is responsible for more than 60 percent of greenhouse gas emissions. As populations continue to grow and more countries begin to industrialize, the demand for energy and other resources will only increase. The current stock of infrastructure will become unsustainable in the long term. This means even more will have to be invested into making existing infrastructure greener and more resilient.[81]

Recent reports have investigated the need for infrastructure as a direct response to these challenges. A joint 2018 study by the United Nations, the World Bank, and the Organization for Economic Cooperation and Development (OECD) projected that $6.3 trillion would have to be invested each year to meet the Sustainable Development Goals. That number climbs to $6.9 to meet the goals of the Paris Agreement. These

---

81 Bhattacharya et al., *Sustainable Infrastructure*, 3.

estimates imply a global infrastructure investment gap of $2.5 to 3 trillion every year.[82]

The need for infrastructure is incredibly great, greater than it has ever been. At the same time, current levels of spending fall woefully short of what is necessary to keep pace with economic growth, much less achieve significant progress in meeting the Sustainable Development Goals and adapting to global crises. If the infrastructure gap is not addressed, the world will only be able to watch as the poorest countries lag further and further behind their peers. One way or another, that gap must be closed, lest our worst fears regarding population growth, urbanization, climate change, conflict, and pandemics become true.

---

[82] OECD/The World Bank/ UN Environment, *Financing Climate Futures*, 20.

3
CLIMATE CHANGE

We are the first generation that can put an end to poverty, and we are the last generation that can put an end to climate change.

—BAN KI-MOON

THINKING ABOUT THE RAIN

The house I grew up in didn't have a basement. It was an old house, the kind mass produced in suburbia during the 1970s. The other houses in my neighborhood were similar, but they all had slight variations in design, perhaps to grant each resident some level of individuality in their choice of a home. Some were red, others blue. A couple here and there were a faded yellow. Most had asphalt driveways but every couple of blocks you would find one made of cement. Each house did however have its own unique mailbox (ours was shaped like a fish).

Some of the houses had basements. I remember being jealous of my friends who had one. A basement wasn't like the rest of a house, especially not for a kid. Every time I was invited over to one of these houses, going into the basement was like being transported to a different world. Basements were the land of pillow forts, junk food, and video games. There was an extra layer of separation between you and the parents. It was the best kind of childhood freedom.

It didn't rain terribly often in Palatine, Illinois, but there were days when the rain would come and wouldn't stop. Those were the days we were stuck inside for indoor recess, reading chapter books and playing board games. One thing that would happen, if it rained enough, was the basements of some of the houses would flood. I remember being utterly confused as to how that could happen, given how the rain was "outside" and the basement was "inside," and yet my friends at school would lament to me about the woes of being trapped out of the basement until the water could be drained. That was the most I ever thought about the rain.

One of my closest friends growing up was the child of Indian immigrants. Later in life, when we started learning more about each other's family histories, he told me about what rain meant to his extended family in India and to so many people in the country. The deepness of the connection between these communities and the weather patterns they experienced was a new concept for me. It was eye-opening to say the least, especially growing up with the kind of tame weather I was accustomed to.

Eighty percent of rainfall in India comes from the yearly monsoon, a seasonal wind that brings with its large changes in precipitation. It blows from the northeast during the cooler months and switches direction to blow from the southwest during the warmer months. As a result, India receives copious amounts of rainfall around June and July. The whole process can turn entire sections of the country from dry deserts to lush, green landscapes. It is absolutely stunning, the differences between two side-by-side photos of certain landscapes in the country just three months apart.[83]

The coming of the monsoon is the most important time of the year. It brings relief from the scorching hot temperatures and revives the parched land until it is teeming with life. Farmers need the monsoon for their agricultural output, on which India's economy is still largely dependent. The monsoon is also of massive cultural significance. From ancient Sanskrit texts to modern Bollywood films, creative endeavors of art, music, and literature have celebrated the change in weather patterns for centuries. Its presence is embodied in myths and legends passed on from generation to generation.[84]

The critical nature of India's relationship to its yearly rainfall cannot be underestimated. That's why now, as the monsoon becomes increasingly unpredictable, unreliable, and dangerous, it is more important than ever to protect that relationship. Something must be done before climate change irreversibly alters the future legacy of the Indian Monsoon and forever changes the way the nation thinks about the rain.[85]

---

83 Ahmaad et al., *Experimental Agrometeorology*, 121.
84 Denton and Sengupta, "India's Ominous Future."
85 Javaheri and Guy, "Historic End."

WHAT'S HAPPENED TO THE RAIN

It isn't uncommon these days to see pedestrian streets transforming into rapidly flowing rivers in many parts of India. Seasonal rains have intensified in recent years, falling for days on end and frequently leading to floods that inundate entire communities. Sewage systems are quickly overwhelmed, and fetid water fills the streets. Residents are forced out of their homes, resorting to living in plastic tent-shelters that provide little protection from the disastrous weather. When the storms finally subside, the displaced wade through waist-high water searching for their lost belongings. In Mumbai, apartment buildings are filled with sludge that takes days to clear out. In Bangalore, plastic and sewage clog up the surrounding lakes, lakes that were once able to contain the excess rain.[86]

Bharati Chaturvedi is the founder of the Chintan Environment Research Group, a non-profit organization that seeks to address issues of sustainability and environmental justice. She describes just how grave the situation has become: "The flood situation in India is absolutely brutal. We've had floods in multiple states, even in Rajasthan in the Jaisalmer district, which is actually a desert."[87]

In September of 2019, the country experienced more monthly rain than it ever had in the past century. From 1950 to 2015, there was a threefold increase in extreme rain events across

---

86   Pai et al., "Daily Rainfall Events."
87   *CAN Insider*, "Flooded by Climate Change."

central India.[88] Imagine the most historically celebrated part of the year turning into a reoccurring natural disaster.

"We have to throw away the prose and poetry written over millennia and start writing new ones!" said Raghu Murtugudde, an Earth systems scientist at the University of Maryland in a 2019 interview with the *New York Times*.[89]

The extreme deluges haven't actually brought with them a greater annual quantity of precipitation. Rainfall in India has become erratic and unpredictable, and total supplies of water are actually decreasing. This means the country is caught in a perpetual cycle of water shortages and flooding. Cherrapunji, a northeastern Indian town, was once the wettest place in the world. In 1974, it set a world record for receiving 24,555 millimeters of rainfall in one year. The town still gets the second most amount of rain in the world, but its levels of precipitation are just one third of what they were only fifty years ago.[90]

Those days of plentiful rain are now history. The droughts and dry spells in between the rainy months have become increasingly intense and protracted. The state of Assam, traditionally known for flooding, has started to experience drought over the past two years. The warmer months can be cruel, dry, and unbearably hot. Wells and reservoirs are constantly depleted, resources that once provided important buffers for drinking water and sanitation between monsoons.

---

88 Roxy et al., "Threefold Rise."
89 Denton and Sengupta, "India's Ominous Future."
90 Bhaumik, "World's Wettest Place."

Many cities have become dependent on tanker trucks that sell limited water supplies from building to building.[91]

Scientists have discovered these radical changes in weather patterns are related to climate change. Record-high temperatures in recent years have impacted the global hydrological cycle, which governs precipitation patterns across the planet. It's behind the increased intensity and unpredictability of the Indian Monsoon.[92]

Here's the science, in a nutshell. Monsoons are caused by differences in temperature between the land and the ocean. Water has a higher heat capacity than dirt, sand, and rocks, meaning its temperature does not change very easily. That's why, on a hot day in early summer, the water at the beach can still be freezing cold. During the warmer months, the sun heats up both the land and the water. The surface of the land quickly rises in temperature. As a result, the air above it rises, and the area becomes a system of low-pressure. At the same time, the ocean is being warmed at a much slower rate, and the air above it becomes a system of high pressure. It is this difference in pressure that causes large sea breezes to blow from the ocean over the surface of India. The winds rise as they enter the low-pressure zones above the land, and the air begins to cool. This decreases the air's water-holding capacity, causing rain to fall. The wind reverses back to the ocean, and the cycle repeats itself.[93]

---

91 Ibid.
92 Roxy et al., "Threefold Rise."
93 Webster and Fasullo, "Tropical Meteorology."

A 2017 study led by the Indian Institute of Tropical Meteorology discovered the rise in extreme rain events over India is caused by increased variability in the westerly winds blowing over the Arabian Sea. The researchers further concluded this increased variability is "linked to the rapid surface warming in the northern Arabian Sea and the adjacent northwest India and Pakistan."[94] The science is proof the floods and droughts are not one-off events. They are related to dramatic changes in the natural environment.[95]

The damages associated with climate hazards like mass flooding speak for themselves, but the numbers are even more daunting. Flooding associated with intense rainfall causes about three billion dollars in annual damages to life, property, and agriculture in India alone. In the last sixty-five years, 268 floods have affected a total of 825 million people. Seventeen million people were rendered homeless at some point during that time, and 69,000 people died. As megacities like Mumbai and Kolkata continue to grow in population, the risk of flood-related damage will only rise.[96]

The analysis has been done. It is no longer a question whether or not climate change is real. If you are skeptical that it is, you are simply lucky enough to live in a part of the world that isn't already experiencing its devastating effects. You don't think about the rain, like I didn't as a child, but know that some people do.

---

94 Roxy et al., "Threefold Rise," 2.
95 Ibid.
96 Ibid.

HEAT THAT CAN KILL YOU

On the opposite side of India's weather spectrum, extreme heat is also wreaking havoc on local economies and human life. During the warmer months, temperatures can climb up to dangerously high levels. In 2019, peak temperatures reached 123 degrees Fahrenheit in the state of Rajasthan, during a heat wave that claimed the lives of thirty-six people.[97]

According to India's National Disaster Management Authority, the number of Indian states that experienced a heat wave rose to nineteen in 2018 from just nine in 2015 and is expected to continue growing. The heat can make people sick. In densely populated cities like New Delhi, the high temperatures bring with them heat stroke, dehydration, and other illnesses. Street vendors collapse from fatigue and nausea. People with fevers and headaches crowd into emergency rooms. Trains without air conditioning sometimes arrive at their destination with fewer people breathing than when they first departed. Over a day's worth of travel being baked inside of a hot car is often the only way for people to travel to work or to visit their families. It's enough to send anyone to the hospital.[98]

Like with flooding, the problem is only going to get worse. The year 2020 was the warmest year ever recorded. The planet's next five warmest years ever were 2015, 2016, 2017, 2018, and, you guessed it, 2019. Nineteen of the warmest years on record have occurred since 2001. The amount of temperature

---

97 Mashal, "India Heat Wave."
98 Ibid.

increase in different locations varies, but the direction our planet is heading is painfully clear.[99]

A 2017 study published in the journal *Science Advances* concluded, at current warming trends, temperatures in South Asia will exceed the threshold of human survivability by the end of the century. The researchers behind the study use the concept of wet bulb temperatures to estimate levels of heat and humidity beyond which the human body will be unable to cool itself. Take a moment to consider what that means. In roughly eighty years, parts of the world will be so hot that without external cooling mechanisms, simply being outside will constitute a life and death situation.[100]

The science, again in a nutshell, is as follows. Wet-bulb temperature is the temperature read by a thermometer covered in a cloth soaked in water. As the water in the cloth evaporates, the thermometer's temperature will decrease relative to the temperature of the air. It is the lowest temperature that can be achieved by evaporation alone.[101] In other words, it's your body's temperature if its only way of cooling down is by sweating. The higher wet-bulb temperatures get, the hotter and more humid it is. When wet-bulb temperatures increase, the difference between the surface temperature of your skin and your inner body temperature decreases. This makes it more difficult for your body to cool itself down. Human beings are incredibly inflexible when it comes to changes in inner body temperature. Any changes above or below one

---

99 NASA, "Global Temperature."
100 Im, Pal, and Eltahir, "Deadly Heat Waves," 1.
101 Razak, *Industrial Gas Turbines*.

degree Celsius can be incredibly dangerous. Inability to regulate this "can immediately impair physical and cognitive functions," according to the *Sciences Advances* paper.[102]

Even the most heat-adapted humans cannot perform normal outdoor functions at wet-bulb temperatures past thirty-two degrees Celsius (ninety degrees Fahrenheit). That's equivalent to a heat index of fifty-five degrees Celsius (130 degrees Fahrenheit), or the temperature that it feels like. The upper physiological limit to human survivability in wet-bulb temperatures is thirty-five degrees Celsius. The maximum amount of time a human can survive in such heat is six hours. Any longer and there is risk of death.[103]

Climate scientists predict parts of South Asia will exceed this threshold of wet-bulb temperatures by the end of the century.[104] What will the people who live there do? Where can they go? As the years go by, asking these questions will become increasingly difficult. Multiple generations of people are alive right now who will live to see the day the earth becomes unlivable.

Until then, the way in which people live their day-to-day lives will progressively change for the worse. A 2018 World Bank book titled, *South Asia's Hotspots,* exampled the long-term effects of changes in temperature and precipitation on living standards in South Asia. The research paints an ominous picture. The current trajectory of climate change will have

---

102 Im, Pal, and Eltahir, "Deadly Heat Waves," 1.
103 Ibid.
104 Ibid.

devastating implications for agricultural output, health, and migration. According to the report, almost half of the entire population of South Asia, more than 800 million people, will be living in locations the book calls "hotspots" by 2050. These are areas where changes in temperatures and precipitation will negatively impact the quality of life.[105]

"With the disruption to the agricultural production, it doesn't need to be the heat wave itself that kills people," says Eltafih Eltahir, one of the authors of the *Science Advances* article. "Production will go down, so potentially everyone will suffer."[106]

None of these climate-related ailments are unique to India. Across the world, entire populations remain incredibly vulnerable to extreme events like droughts, heatwaves, and floods. And the sick reality is the poorest countries will unequivocally be the most affected. As of 2021, several countries in Southern Africa are still suffering through a debilitating drought that began over two years ago.[107] There are already forty-five million people in Africa who struggle every day to find food. Unpredictable weather patterns, similar to the variability in the Indian monsoon, can wipe out an entire year's worth of crop yield and cause widespread famine.[108]

---

105 Mani et al., *South Asia's Hotspots*, 9-10.
106 Chandler, "Deadly Heat Waves."
107 Carlowicz, "Drought Threatens Millions."
108 Anyadike, "Drought in Africa."

THE CLIMATE CRISIS AND SUSTAINABLE INFRASTRUCTURE

The Paris Agreement in 2015 was a monumental moment in which the countries of the world came together and committed to keeping global temperature increases well below two degrees Celsius. The focus of these accords was on stopping climate change at its root. It was part of the effort to halt, or even reverse, the underlying causes of global warming. Unfortunately, as is painfully clear in far too many countries, the climate crisis is already with us. The Earth isn't going to stop heating up before permanent damage is dealt. While the rich, developed countries slowly contemplate whether or not their carbon footprint is worth a marginal drop in bottom-line performance, the poorest will suffer existential consequences.

Consider the following statement from the sixth edition of the United Nation's *Global Environment Outlook*.

"Climate change has become an independent driver of environmental change. Regardless of human action, or even human presence on the planet, impacts will continue to occur through temperature change, fluctuations of precipitation, snow melt, sea level rise, drought, and other climate variables, and through changes in the hydrological cycle. Climate change thus poses a challenge to growth and development."[109]

Anthropogenic climate change has already been built into this planet's future due to centuries of past emissions. Because of inertia in the climate and carbon cycle, even if humanity

---

109 UN Environment, *Global Environment Outlook*, 44.

were to completely erase its carbon footprint today, future generations will still suffer the consequences. That means the time has passed for us to bicker about how our planet ended up here in the first place. Whether it was humanity's greed, capitalism, or ill-fated destiny, the results are the same. People are in danger. This is the reality of climate change we face.

In light of this inevitability, the policy agenda on climate change must shift from being purely focused on reversal to also considering adaptation and mitigation. Action must be taken now to help countries manage extreme weather events, rising temperatures, natural resource destruction, and ecological degradation. Resilience must be built up in the most vulnerable regions of the world. The ability of countries to handle climate-related challenges will dictate their entire futures. Failure to do so will eradicate any hope for progress and prosperity for billions of people.

One of the most potent responses to this challenge involves climate-resistant and sustainable infrastructure. It reflects how current infrastructure will be affected by climate change and how new infrastructure can be built to prepare for, adapt to, and mitigate those effects. The following sections will explore some of the political, environmental, and economic dimensions that sustainable infrastructure can impact as well as practical ways for countries to scale up commitments to climate resilience.

PROTECTING RESOURCES IN A CHANGING CLIMATE
Some of the greatest climate-related challenges countries face today are exacerbated, if not enabled, by low quality or

lack of infrastructure. Water is particularly important, being the primary resource affected by climate change. Sustainable and climate-resistant infrastructure can be a means to increase water efficiency, protect water supply, and defend against floods.

Take the droughts and shortages in Bangalore for example. The South Indian city boasts a population of twelve million and has become a rapidly growing hub of technology and innovation. Older Bangaloreans will tell you the city once sat on land surrounded by clean lakes. The lakes held rainwater during the dry months and served as an important source of water for the city. Rapid urbanization and building expansion completely changed that. These days, the lakes are filled to the brim with plastic waste and sewage. Many of them were destroyed or built over to make room for residential areas, golf courses, and corporate campuses.[110]

Now, despite its major metropolitan status, Bangalore has no reliable water source of its own. Instead, it must pump water from the distant Kaveri River. It's an incredibly expensive and inefficient task. The river lies over ninety miles away and 900 feet below the city. Transporting water costs six million dollars a month in electricity, and over 20 percent of it is lost due to leaks in the old and corroded pipe infrastructure. When the water actually reaches the city, it isn't properly distributed to every citizen. About a quarter of Bangalore's population is unconnected to a water main. Even those with access to piped water often turn on their taps to find a mere

---

110 Banerji, "Bengaluru Water Crisis."

trickle. Both are clear indications of the underdevelopment of water infrastructure.[111]

Though it wouldn't completely erase them, higher-quality piping systems and more connections to the water grid would solve some of the supply problems Bangalore is facing. It would make the city more efficient at transporting its water resources to as many people as possible. But climate change is here, and natural supplies of water are dwindling. The Kaveri River is shrinking and the groundwater unconnected citizens rely on is nearly exhausted. One solution is to harvest more rainwater. Though monsoon rains are gradually declining and becoming more erratic, a substantial amount still falls over Bangalore. The city gets somewhere around 800 milliliters of rain in a year. If it were to catch and store half of that, it would amount to more than one hundred liters (twenty-seven gallons) per person per day, which would substantially enhance the city's water security.[112]

Doing so would require building a new kind of infrastructure called, recharge wells. These wells would recycle a large portion of rain into groundwater. During the monsoon months, the groundwater underneath the city would be rapidly replenished. Currently, because of the way pavement is laid out, only 10 percent of rainwater can seep down into the aquifers below. A system of recharge wells could increase that number up to 60 percent and make a monumental difference in the city's water supply.[113]

---

111 Ibid.
112 Kumar-Rao, "India's Water Crisis."
113 Ibid.

Water shortages in Bangalore illustrate how climate change can put pressures on both the supply and demand of resources. As extreme weather and environmental degradation drive more people to urban centers, the demand for water, sanitation, and irrigation services will continue to go up. At the same time, reservoirs and other natural sources of water may dry out under increasingly high temperatures and erratic precipitation may prevent them from being recharged, causing the cost of providing those services to also rise. The same goes for energy. People will demand more electricity for air-conditioning during the hot summer months at the same time grids struggle to operate under extreme conditions. Sustainable infrastructure investments in resource-stressed areas will be critical to keeping pace with these shifts.

CLIMATE-RESILIENT INFRASTRUCTURE

Infrastructure assets themselves can be at serious risk of climate-related disruptions. Both new and old infrastructure systems will be more vulnerable to breaking down when faced with extreme temperatures and weather events. Pipes in water mains can burst in the freezing cold. Roads and railways can break down in extreme heat. Coastal infrastructure can be inundated by rising sea levels. Both storms and droughts can shut down power plants and cause power outages, rendering other systems like water treatment inoperable. In 2011, flooding in the Zhejiang and Hubei provinces of China damaged and disrupted twenty-eight rail links, 21,961 roads, forty-nine airports, and 8,516 electricity transmission lines.[114]

---

114 Hu, "Chinese Infrastructure."

The problem isn't unique to emerging economies. In February of 2021, severe winter storms and record low temperatures caused power outages throughout Texas, leaving millions of residents to suffer in the cold without heating. The arctic weather caused several power plants to freeze over and go offline, causing a massive shortfall in electricity supply at the same time demand skyrocketed. Not only was power cut off from individual homes and businesses, but the state's water treatment plants were also inoperable without electricity, and seven million Texans were ordered by public officials to conserve and boil their water for safe use. Situations like this can be incredibly dangerous and even life threatening to those without the right preparations and equipment.[115]

Researchers estimate that most of the physical damage caused by extreme weather events will be borne by infrastructure sectors. The disruptions in water, energy, transport, communications services can wreak havoc on economic and living conditions. For example, climate-related damage to transport infrastructure could disrupt global supply chains and food production, increasing the risk of price swings and food insecurity. OECD modeling of flood scenarios in Paris showed up to 55 percent of flood damages would be borne by infrastructure sectors and up to 85 percent of business losses would be caused by disruptions to transport and electricity. In this sense, resilient infrastructure *is* climate resilience.[116]

In Africa, drought has the potential to cause river basins to dry out, a situation that could wipe out critical sources of

---

[115] Romo, "Millions in Texas."
[116] OECD, *Climate-resilient Infrastructure*, 15.

hydropower. A book published by the World Bank on the state of climate resilience in Africa's infrastructure found that "failure to integrate climate change in the planning and design of power and water infrastructure could entail, in scenarios of drying climate conditions, losses of hydropower revenues between 5 percent and 60 percent (depending on the basin) and increases in consumer expenditure for energy up to three times the corresponding baseline values."[117]

These examples illustrate the water-energy nexus that forms the heart of the climate crisis. Both systems are mutually dependent on one another. Water and wastewater treatment plants can't function properly without electricity. Energy grids can't function without water for cooling and hydropower. Vulnerability to climate change isn't driven by the risk in individual assets, but by the system as a whole. The interconnectedness of infrastructure may lead to a domino effect in terms of disruption, but it also presents the opportunity for infrastructure sectors to mutually reinforce their resilience. A stronger water sector leads to a stronger energy sector, and vice versa.

How exactly, then, can infrastructure design account for these risks? An obvious response involves locating assets in areas at lower risk of climate-related hazards. The further away physical structures underlying infrastructure systems are from zones prone to flooding events, the less likely they are to be shut down during storms. Structural adjustments can also help assets adapt to environmental changes. For example, raising the height of bridges to account for changes

---

[117] Cervigni et al., *Enhancing Climate Resilience*.

in sea-level or building roads with heat-resistant materials to prevent them from cracking in extremely high temperatures. These adaptations will increase the lifespan of assets and maintain the reliability of service provision. The long-term nature of infrastructure is such that design features now will have implications for many years to come.

Other assets like cyclone shelters and coastal embankments can respond directly to weather disasters such as flooding and storm surges. Ecosystem-based infrastructure can be built directly in the environment. Natural drainage systems, for example, can be used to manage stormwater and preserve wetlands. Watershed restoration can inhibit the contamination of drinking water sources. These "green" approaches are often cheaper than built infrastructure and can go a long way toward minimizing ecological damage.

The potential benefits of incorporating climate-resilience into infrastructure design are wide-ranging. The OECD identifies the following in its 14th Policy Perspectives report, *Climate-Resilient Infrastructure*:[118]

- Increased reliability of service provision: Reliable infrastructure has benefits ex-post, by reducing the frequency and severity of disruption. It also has benefits ex-ante, as it reduces the need for users to invest in backup measures (e.g., generators for businesses).
- Increased asset life, reduced repair and maintenance costs: Preparing for climate change at the outset can avoid

---

118 OECD, *Climate-resilient Infrastructure*, 9.

the need for costly retrofitting and reduce the risk of the asset becoming prematurely obsolete.
- Increased efficiency of service provision: In some cases, considering the impacts of climate change can reduce the unit costs of providing a service relative to business-as-usual approaches, for example through better management of hydropower resources.
- Co-benefits: Some approaches to climate-resilient infrastructure, particularly the use of natural infrastructure, can deliver an equivalent service to traditional approaches while also generating co-benefits such as amenity value, biodiversity conservation, and climate change mitigation.

A few notable examples exist of cities successfully preparing for climate change through targeted investments in infrastructure. Hong Kong, for example, is heavily prone to tropical cyclones. With an average annual rainfall of around 24,000 millimeters per year, it's one of the wettest cities in the world. It's also one of the most densely populated cities, and its citizens have historically been highly vulnerable to flood damage. With both torrential rains and sea levels on the rise, the city has sought to improve its climate resilience.[119]

The Drainage Services Department of Hong Kong pioneered a stormwater management system that it calls, "Sponge City." The essential idea is to absorb and store water during wet seasons and reuse it to meet water and sanitation needs throughout the city. Urban environments throughout the world are typically prone to high surface runoffs because water can't sink into concrete and pavement. The "sponge" approach,

---

119 Drainage Services Department, "Sponge City."

however, involves a network of infrastructure that mimics nature by enabling high evaporation, high infiltration, and a low surface runoff. Green roofs and porous pavements allow rainwater to be collected and stored for future use. Flood retention lakes and riverside parks are designed as both scenic sites for public enjoyment and as a mechanism to contain floods. As a result of its initiatives, Hong Kong has minimized its vulnerability to weather-related hazards. From 1995 to 2017, the number of areas at risk of severe flood damage have fallen from ninety to just seven.[120]

MANAGING CLIMATE RISK

The unpredictable and variable nature of climate change makes planning for resilient infrastructure difficult and expensive. Though climate risk as a whole is certainly increasing, quantifying exact climate risk for individual locations and assets is still incredibly challenging. The extent of risk depends on local weather and geographic conditions. What constitutes resilience for one road or reservoir may not be applicable to another. Climate and weather modeling can give us an idea of areas that are more or less vulnerable but predicting specific outcomes with exact probability is unlikely.

Time horizons for when climate resilient features will come into play are also difficult to estimate. Rising sea levels, increasing temperatures, and different weather events will not occur at the same time nor at the same rate. It may be more necessary to respond immediately to certain hazards

---

120 Ibid.

than others. These uncertainties can be alleviated to an extent by higher-quality data and more accurate projections, but fully predicting the future is an impossible task.

Climate risk is also amplified by local socioeconomic conditions and trends that are also hard to quantify. Water supply risk depends on changes in water demand, which depends on population growth and urbanization. Climate change will also interact in unpredictable ways with global development challenges like poverty, inequality, the pandemic, and conflict and fragility. Gender equality, in particular, has important implications for the effectiveness of resilient infrastructure solutions. Threats to local water supplies can further disenfranchise women who disproportionately shoulder the burden of collecting water. Piped water and sanitation services can support female empowerment, provide more economic opportunities, and lower the risk of sexual assault.[121]

To account for these complexities in their investment and policy decisions, global leaders will need access to high quality information and platforms capable of capitalizing on that information. Greater investments in environmental analysis and climate modeling can minimize the risk of preparing for hazards that won't materialize. Increasingly sophisticated datasets can inform solutions that can be implemented according to circumstances at the national, state, and local level. For example, Argentina developed an interactive tool called the Climate Change Risk Maps System (SIMARCC) that uses georeferenced data to map out levels of climate risk

---

[121] OECD, *Climate-resilient Infrastructure*, 7.

and social vulnerability across the country. The tool is being used to shape public policies and infrastructure programs related to climate adaptation.[122]

Even more so than these analytical tools, our world needs to muster the political, economic, and social will to build climate resilience. If the present actions of our global leaders are any indication, we are still very much not taking the climate crisis as seriously as we need to. Nine out of ten of the world's biggest emitters of carbon dioxide are not on pace to bring their emissions down to the levels necessary to keep warming below two degrees Celsius.[123] Every year is getting warmer than the last. Heat waves and tropical storms are happening more frequently, and the cost to human life and well-being is accelerating. The need to respond to these challenges has never been greater, yet infrastructure in even the most developed countries is deteriorating and are vulnerable.[124]

Many tools of innovation are at our disposal today, both in terms of the engineering required to build infrastructure sustainability and the financial instruments needed to attract enough money to pay for it. It is on us to use those tools and take responsibility for the damage humanity has unleashed onto the environment and the damage the environment will unleash back onto us. Hope is not yet lost for all of us sitting precipice of climate disaster. Infrastructure, *sustainable* infrastructure, will be an indispensable part of keeping hope alive.

---

122 PPPLRC, "Argentina's Climate Risks."
123 Akpan, "Climate Pledges."
124 Fountain, "Irreversible Change."

4

COOKING

I love to watch my mother cook. She's a mastermind in the kitchen, capable of fashioning complex dishes out of innumerable ingredients. She handles knives and utensils like an orchestra conductor with a baton, composing a symphony of flavors somehow in utter disarray and complete order at the same time. She uses techniques and recipes hundreds of years old while incorporating inventions and methods of her own. I could never wrap my head around how she always got the timing right. Five dishes, all beginning at different times but always ending together. It was meticulous yet effortless. You could tell just how much pure intuition was built over decades of practice. Sitting there and watching, it's easy to miss all the important details. A pinch of seasoning here. A little less heat there. You couldn't write it all down in a cookbook.

As is the case with many Asian cultures, my mom showed her love for us through her food. I grew up getting served a mix of traditional Chinese food alongside an immigrant's take on classic American dishes, plus a few experimental meals here and there to encourage a more diverse palate. I could eat soup dumplings for breakfast, seafood pasta for lunch, and barbecue ribs for dinner. As corny as it sounds, you could taste that she cared. One of my first encounters with the idea of privilege happened when my friends invited me over to have dinner at their house. I enjoyed it for the novelty, but dinner at home was on another level. The other moms at our community church would come up to me after Sunday service and poke fun at how "lucky" I was. They weren't wrong. My mom's dishes were always finished first at the family potlucks.

My mom was born in Tongzhou, a small district in the eastern province of Jiangsu, China. At that time, China was still one of the poorest countries in the world. Most people still subsisted off small-scale agriculture, and many died because they couldn't. My mom's family had a small, stone house and a tiny patch of land in the rural outskirts of the town where they could grow vegetables and raise a few animals. To this day, that piece of land belongs to them, and they call it the "old home."

My grandfather had a job as a cook in a large public cafeteria. The food he made in the government's kitchen wasn't the kind of bland, average food we associate with cafeterias today. It was specially made for the white-collar workers of the Communist Party, and they ate well. There was stir-fried meat dishes, steamed fish, deep fried vegetables, and other foods the typical Tongzhou resident would only eat on rare, special occasions.

There weren't many roads in rural China during the 1970s, so my grandfather lived apart from his family in the city where he worked. He would make the long trip back home a few times each month to bring money and some goods that could only be bought in the city. Sometimes, he would bring home a small container full of whatever was being served at the cafeteria that day. The food would have traveled over two hours on bike with him, but even the cold, beat-up form it arrived in was a special treat for the family. As my mom recalls, opening that box was like opening a present. You couldn't wait to find out what was inside. You could pretend to be one of the rich city folks who ate whatever they wanted, if only for the short moment between biting and swallowing.

Eating at home in Tongzhou wasn't quite the same. The food my mom grew up eating wasn't luxurious by any means, and it was scarce. Most meals were some combination of rice porridge and whatever vegetables were growing in the garden. Because of my grandfather's job, their family fared relatively well compared to some of the other folks in the rural areas. Many simply had nothing to eat when crops weren't in season or when yield was low. Back then, the long winter months in Tongzhou brought with them the full force of extreme poverty, and many lives were lost to starvation. At the very least, as my mom remembers, their family always had enough rice stored away to stave off the kind of prolonged hunger happening in some of the homes around them.

The food they did have had to be cooked at home, but cooking back then was a completely different process from what my mom does today. In a corner of her childhood home, there was a traditional wood-burning stove. It consisted of a wide concrete countertop that protruded from the wall about two feet off the ground and a hollowed-out chamber underneath where you would put firewood or coal. On top, there was a half-sphere-shaped cavity where you would place a wok. The wok was an all-purpose tool that serviced all types of cooking, from boiling and steaming to sautéing and frying. In the mornings, before my mother walked to school, she would go out into the fields to pick up twigs, branches, and dried vegetation to serve as fuel for that day's fire. Electricity and gas connections had not yet arrived in rural China at that point, so most people still relied on burning wood, charcoal, animal waste, or crop residue to cook their food.

When my mom and her parents were boiling water or cooking, smoke would rise from the fire chamber (as is the case when you burn any kind of wood and coal). A narrow, chimney-like structure would funnel the smoke outside. The house itself wasn't sealed or insulated very well, so the smoke that didn't make it through the chimney would eventually find its way out through the cracks. But there were days when the smoke lingered, and my mother had to stay outside to avoid breathing in the toxic fumes. The walls in that corner of the kitchen were stained black with soot and smoke residue. They didn't think about cooking as a direct threat to health back then, but that's what it was. You had to start a fire in order to cook, and you could only start a fire with materials that would produce smoke.

By the time my mother had access to a stove that wasn't powered by biomass fuels, she had already finished graduate school and was working full time at an environmental planning agency in the growing city of Nanjing. Natural gas pipelines were still incredibly scarce in China, but many of the urban homes started having stoves that could be connected to liquified petroleum gas (LPG) canisters. Aside from being able to control temperature and cook at a moment's notice, the greatest difference LPG made was how much less polluting the gas stoves were compared to traditional stoves. Less smoke and soot particles were emitted, and the walls around the stove would stay roughly the same color.

Hundreds of millions of people in China have since gained access to similar cooking mechanisms, with the country growing in national income and living standards.[125] But across the world, the vast majority of people in low-income, developing countries still depend on solid fuels like animal dung, agricultural waste, wood, and coal. These fuel sources are either burned over open fires or in traditional stoves made of stone and clay. They also happen to be deadly.[126]

A GLOBAL HEALTH CRISIS SITTING RIGHT IN OUR HOMES

Traditional fuels have very low energy content and are incredibly inefficient. Fuelwood, for example, has an energy content of 16 MJ/kg when burned in a traditional stove. Dung has even less at 14.5 MJ/kg. In comparison, modern fuels like kerosene and LPG have energy contents of 43 MJ/kg and 45.5 MJ/kg, respectively.[127] In other words, a lot more traditional fuel has to be used to generate an equivalent amount of heat. Cooking even the simplest meal can also take hours of time and effort gathering fuelwood or shoveling dung.

---

125 Bhattacharyya and Ohiare, "Chinese Electricity."
126 WHO, "Household Air Pollution."
127 Malla and Timilsina, "Household Cooking Fuel Choice," 10-11.

Cooking with traditional fuels can also be incredibly detrimental to health outcomes. Humans have been using wood to start fires and heat food for over a million years.[128] In some ways, it seems odd to think of such a tried-and-true practice as being incredibly dangerous, but it is. Traditional fuels produce high levels of air pollution and soot particles that can cause serious damage when inhaled into the lungs. In small, poorly ventilated spaces, where most of the world's poor live, indoor air pollution is a very serious problem.[129] Imagine having to cook over a campfire in your living room multiple times a day.

Dorothy Uwamariya used to spend entire days gathering firewood. She's a young mother from a rural village in Rwanda. Like millions of other women in Africa, the task of cooking and preparing meals has fallen on her shoulders. With very limited means of starting a fire, feeding the family can be a long and arduous process. For many people across Africa, wood and charcoal produced from the wood are the primary sources of fuel for cooking. The continent's use of charcoal comprises 63 percent of the world's total consumption. "Cooking with charcoal was difficult for me. It wasn't fast enough to get meals ready for the kids, and my small house was always filled with smoke," said Dorothy. During rainy months, she had no choice but to cook inside, where her family would breathe in the polluted air caused by the fire.[130]

---

128 Cohen, "Human Ancestors."
129 WHO, "Household Air Pollution."
130 *Sustainable Energy for All*, "Clean Cooking in Rwanda."

The relationship between a household's choice of cooking fuel and various socioeconomic factors is well established. The lower household income is, the more likely a family is to use traditional fuels. As income rises, the utilization of cleaner, more efficient fuels increases. Other factors like the level of education of the heads of households, particularly women, also have a significant effect on the use of traditional cooking fuel. But this should come as no surprise.[131] Like many of the world's greatest challenges, the burden of unclean cooking falls exclusively on the shoulders of the poor.

It wouldn't be an exaggeration to say the lack of clean cooking methods poses one of the greatest threats to human health in the world today. A laundry list of toxic air compounds is released due to the combustion of traditional cooking fuels, including carbon monoxide, polyaromatic hydrocarbons, benzene, and formaldehyde. Toxic particles like ash, sulfur, and mercury are also emitted. These pollutants cause inflammation in the lungs and reduce the oxygen carrying capacity of an individual's blood. Exposure is also related to increased incidents of illnesses like stroke, pneumonia, heart disease, and lung cancer. These illnesses cause four million premature deaths every single year, according to the World Health Organization.[132]

In 2013, over 200 researchers collaborated on a study seeking to identify the biggest risk factors for disease across the entire globe. They concluded that household air pollution from solid fuels was the third greatest risk factor, behind only

---

131 Malla and Timilsina, "Household Cooking Fuel Choice," 11-12.
132 WHO, "Household Air Pollution."

tobacco smoking and high blood pressure. For women, it is the second most important risk factor. In South Asia, household air pollution is the single greatest risk factor for disease burden.[133] Studies of women in India and Nepal who cook using traditional fuels show death rates due to respiratory illness similar to those of heavy smokers.[134]

As COVID-19, a respiratory illness, rampages through the planet, this health crisis already of astronomical proportions, has become even more serious. The spread and mortality rate of the virus is heavily influenced by underlying health conditions. The diseases influenced by exposure to household air pollution are the very ones that complicate and increase the severity of a coronavirus infection.[135]

These burdens are disproportionately borne by women and young children who spend the most time around cookstoves. Fuel-gathering takes away hours every week from women and children, limiting time for education and other productive activities. Half of the four million premature deaths caused by indoor air pollution are children under the age of five.[136] To complicate matters further, cooking with nonrenewable biomass is a heavy contributor to global emissions and climate change. A gigaton of carbon dioxide could be removed from the air if cookstoves were cleaner.[137]

---

133 Lim et al., "Comparative Risk Assessment."
134 Modi et al., *Energy Services*.
135 Mbungu, "Lack of Clean Cooking."
136 WHO, "Household Air Pollution."
137 Bailis et al., "Carbon Footprint," 269.

"Lack of progress in clean cooking is costing the world more than $2.4 trillion each year, driven by adverse impacts on health, climate, and gender equality," said Makhtar Diop, vice president of infrastructure at the World Bank.[138]

Exposure is also linked to impairments in child development, including poor cognitive functioning, low birthweight, and childhood stunting. The disruption of a child's natural growth and development is absolutely no joke. It has serious consequences, not only for the child, but for the health and wellbeing of entire nations.[139]

Even if access to education is improved, children stunted by malnourishment and toxic environments when they are young will be impossibly disadvantaged when it comes to competing in the global economy. Scientists have discovered that these children literally have fewer neuronal connections in their brains, which severely impairs their ability to learn.[140] That doesn't bode well for a future that is undergoing rapid technological change and that increasingly demands a skilled and educated workforce. These days, it is nearly impossible to find a job if you don't know how to use a computer in developed countries. As automation and artificial intelligence take away more and more agricultural and service jobs, this will become increasingly true in developing countries. To say nothing of access to technology, imagine what it will be like for entire populations who have no hope of learning how to use it. It is a massive problem that will keep poor nations

---

138 Clean Cooking Alliance, "New Report."
139 Islam and Mohanty, "Maternal Exposure."
140 Xie et al., "Growth Faltering."

forever poor. Thirty-eight percent of children are stunted in India.[141] Forty-three percent are stunted in sub-Saharan Africa.[142] It's a problem with the potential to rob a country of its future.

"This is probably the root of intergenerational poverty," said Jim Yong Kim, a previous president of the World Bank.[143]

CLEAN COOKING

The path to clean cooking is obviously related to the problem of fuel and electricity access, but the problem is more widespread than you may think. Cooking is an incredibly unique phenomenon rooted in cultural traditions and local contexts. How a household cooks and what they use to cook with depends on the individual user's needs and preferences. Convenience or habit may also cause families to simply choose not to use cleaner cooking solutions that may be available to them.

In September of 2020, Loughborough University and the World Bank's Energy Sector Management Assistance Program (ESMAP) published a joint report titled *The State of Access to Modern Energy Cooking Service*. Using a 71-country sample of 5.3 billion people, the report estimated four billion people "lack the ability to cook efficiently, cleanly, conveniently, reliably, safely, and affordably." That's roughly half of the world population. Access, as always, varies by region.

---

141 Banerjee et al., "Disparity in Childhood Stunting," 2.
142 Keino et al., "Determinants of Stunting," 2.
143 Boseley, "World Bank to Name."

In sub-Saharan Africa, only 10 percent of the population has access to modern energy cooking solutions. Latin America and East Asia fare better comparatively, at 56 percent and 36 percent, respectively.[144]

In recent years, access to cleaner cookstoves and cleaner fuels has been improving in rapidly growing countries like India and China, where rising incomes and urbanization have improved access to cleaner fuels and energy infrastructure. In Africa, however, little to no improvement has been made. In fact, the situation has been deteriorating. Between 1990 and 2011, consumption of biomass in Africa grew by an average of 2.6 percent every year. Access to clean cooking has only marginally increased since 2015 and has been outpaced by population growth, meaning the total number of people who rely on solid fuels is actually going up.[145]

The extent of this particular deficit betrays its complexity. If you recall, the global population without access to electricity is around 770 million, meaning billions of electricity users still lack access to clean cooking. Even as the number of households with electricity connections has grown, so too has the number of households cooking with wood, charcoal, and coal. Despite decades of awareness of the issue, little progress has been made, and, without significant investments and policy changes, the situation will remain largely unchanged.[146]

---

144 ESMAP, *State of Access*, 35.
145 Malla and Timilsina, "Household Cooking Fuel Choice," 4-5.
146 Energy Sector Management Assistance Program (ESMAP), *State of Access*, 37.

The problem of unclean cooking illustrates not only what energy infrastructure can solve, but also what it can't. From a health and environmental perspective, the ideal situation would be to produce and distribute more clean, renewable energy and supply people with modern fuel stoves. But these solutions are complicated, expensive, and long term. Very little attention has been drawn to electricity as a clean cooking solution because so many rural communities lack electricity.[147]

Buying an expensive electric or biogas stove is also hardly an attractive option for families who are used to using cheap and readily available traditional fuels. World Bank estimates show these stoves are affordable to under 20 to 30 percent of households in most countries in Asian and Africa. Furthermore, cleaner stoves may not fit into culturally significant methods of cooking and preparing food.[148]

With the health crisis associated with unclean cooking already so extensive, there isn't time to wait for countries to build more energy capacity. Cooking is an everyday necessity, so interim solutions must be scaled up in the meantime.

I recently spoke with Shrikant Avi, senior manager at The Clean Cooking Alliance, about off-grid solutions for clean cooking.

"It will be a long time before grid-connected solutions for clean cooking become prevalent, especially in Africa," he

---

147 ESMAP, *State of Access*, 44.
148 Ibid.

said. "The expansion of grid infrastructure and the affordability of related cooking solutions will be key drivers in expanding access to electric cooking. While a lot of research and development is currently being conducted to develop such solutions, there is an argument to also support the scaling of alternate, transitional solutions."

For the last three years, Shrikant has been helping companies in the clean cooking space raise capital and scale their operations through grants and technical assistance programs. In 2019, he visited one such company in Cambodia that supplied piped biogas directly to rural farmers in exchange for their animal waste. Biogas is produced from the breakdown of organic material through a process called anaerobic digestion. Cooking with it is significantly less polluting and environmentally hazardous than cooking with traditional fuels.[149]

"Instead of throwing away the animal waste, the farmers use it to run the biogas plant, which can save a lot of money and energy," said Srikant.

Other countries have focused more on propane-based technologies like liquid petroleum gas (LPG). LPG is derived from the oil refinement process and can be used for common household appliances and cooking. It comes in large, pressurized steel canisters, often seen connected to the sides of houses. Like biogas, LPG is also much cleaner and more energy efficient than traditional fuels. It produces very little

---

149 Tanigawa, "Biogas."

smoke and air pollutants, and, with the right stove, combustion ends right when you want it to.[150]

In May of 2018, Dorothy was able to purchase a modernized cookstove that runs on LPG. It's relatively simple, by some measures: a small black box about four inches tall with nothing more than two burners and two knobs. Sitting on a thin wooden platform under the winder in her home, the stove represents a monumental shift in the family's lifestyle.

"Before that, I used to struggle to cook for the kids," she said.

The improvements in health effects from switching to cleaner fuels are significant. Anders Ellegård, a professor of human ecology at the University of Göthard, discovered users of fuelwood in Mozambique were exposed to levels of toxic particles six times that of LPG users.[151] Researchers at UC Berkeley and the International Clinical Epidemiology Network studied the impact of the use of different cooking fuels on infants in India and concluded the use of LPG was associated with significantly lower risk of low birth weight and neonatal death (death within the first twenty-eight days of birth).[152] Another experiment in Nigeria showed pregnant women who made the switch exhibited significant reductions in blood pressure levels.[153]

The expansion of LPG penetration in places like Africa, however, is heavily limited by an underdeveloped infrastructure.

---

150 Puzzolo et al., "Supply Considerations," 373-374.
151 Ellegård, "Cooking Fuel Smoke."
152 Epstein et al., "Household Fuels."
153 Alexander et al., "Ethanol Cookstove Intervention."

The distribution process requires bulk storage terminals and filling plants where the fuel is moved into canisters as well as adequate roads to move the fuel to residential areas.[154] This means investing heavily in infrastructure will be a necessary pre-condition even for interim solutions. Without it, there will be little hope for either government and multilateral initiatives or private businesses to achieve the scale necessary to reach the number of people in need.

Still, at the end of the day, LPG is a fossil fuel, and fossil fuel-based solutions are temporary by nature. They also don't completely remove the effects of pollution and carbon emissions. As important as interim cooking solutions are to remedying this global health crisis, countries will soon need to invest in long-term, sustainable options. Large-scale renewable energy infrastructure like solar and wind will need to be developed to meet energy needs far into the future.

It won't be an easy task, by any means. Renewables are still evolving as an industry and investing in solar and wind is difficult even in advanced economies. It wouldn't be farfetched to doubt their potential in helping to achieve universal energy access—nor is it necessarily fair to ask developing countries to forgo fossil-fuels when countries like the US primarily use gas-based cooking.[155]

"Several investors are evaluating the funding of LPG projects under the current global context where there is a meaningful shift towards renewable energy," said Shrikant. "The

---

154 Puzzolo et al., "Supply Considerations," 373-374.
155 US Energy Information Administration, "Natural Gas Explained."

argument for LPG investment in cooking is often justified as investment in a transitional fuel while renewable solutions may become viable over time."

As unfair and difficult as it may be, the clean cooking problem is not one that can be avoided, and there may not be time even for some transitional technologies. Scaling up sustainable energy infrastructure must be the path forward.

5

CONFLICT

THIRSTY FOR CHANGE

Anyone would've made the same mistake.

A mother and her child are sitting at the base of a tree on a sweltering day. No human being would see them there and assume anything more than their desire to escape the heat by resting in the shade. That's exactly what Mary, a twenty-five-year-old woman from South Sudan thought, as she walked past them on her way to the local water pump. But on second look, she saw neither of the bodies were moving. They had both died from dehydration.[156]

Mary, a mother herself, is from Gumuruq, a rural village in the South Sudanese state of Boma. It's a remote place only accessible by helicopter, with dirt track roads extending to and from the village being insufficient for long distances. Like many of the other women from Gumuraq, it's Mary's responsibility to retrieve water supplies for her family. The

---

156 Trew, "South Sudan."

nearest functioning water pump is eight hours away by foot.[157]

As laborious and time-consuming as the trip is, we've already established that her task isn't particularly unique. Across Africa, millions of women must embark on similar treks in search of safe drinking water.[158] But Mary's task is complicated by an additional factor, one that might explain the mother and child she saw at the tree: violence.

From 2013 to 2020, South Sudan was plagued by a brutal civil war that claimed the lives of almost 400,000 people.[159] The remnants of the protracted conflict between the government and rebel groups still haunt the everyday lives of citizens. At the heart of this unrest is South Sudan's intense water insecurity. According to the government's water authority, 80 percent of the world's youngest country lacks access to clean water.[160] Most citizens rely on blue tanker trucks that drive around selling water to various towns and villages without better options. But the truck routes can be erratic, and often the cost of fuel prohibits them from traveling to the remote areas on the outskirts of larger cities. On those days, when the trucks are nowhere to be seen, people wait in line for hours at water pumps and boreholes to get a chance at fetching untreated water.[161]

---

157 Ibid.
158 Hallett, "Millions of Women."
159 Reuters, "South Sudan's Civil War."
160 Ritter, "South Sudanese Dying."
161 Glinski, "Price of Water."

The dwindling supply of life's most essential resource has continued to spark competition and conflict among the country's different ethnic groups. As a result, women like Mary find themselves caught in a deadly crossfire. In addition to the risk of dying from hunger or thirst on her long trips, she has to be wary of being ambushed and assaulted by men looking to steal the precious water in her jerrycan. Some women are threatened at gunpoint.[162]

"We have all been attacked walking to the boreholes," said Mary in 2019. The scars that run up and down her legs are a testament to the flogging she experienced at the hands of several men. Her recovery took a full ten months. "Since that time until now, I am too weak to get water."[163]

The conflicts ignited by the water crisis don't end there. Climate change has caused seasonal rivers to dry up earlier than anticipated, forcing many cattle herding communities to migrate in search of water. The movement of these shepherding groups has increased the number of raids on their cattle stock, further fueling the tension between rival groups.[164]

"Water creates real armed conflicts among the pastoral communities, particularly as the dry season gets longer," said Alier Ngongoka, chair of the South Sudanese water authority.[165]

---

162 Trew, "South Sudan."
163 Ibid.
164 Ibid.
165 Ibid.

What's worse, cattle-raids go hand-in-hand with child abductions. Raiders have made a business out of kidnapping children in addition to livestock and selling them to families unable to conceive on their own.[166]

All this because there isn't enough water.

But conflicts over water resources in the Sudanese region aren't anything new. In fact, these incidents in South Sudan are mere skirmishes in comparison to the larger wars fought in decades past. The War in Darfur and the Second Sudanese Civil War fought between the North and the South before they were separate nations were also influenced in many ways by water insecurity. Between 1972 and 1983, after the First Sudanese Civil War, South Sudan, still a part of the whole of Sudan, experienced a period of stability and socioeconomic progress. Ecologically, South Sudan is much wetter and more fertile than the North. It has access to the large drainage basins of the White and Blue Niles in addition to steady rainfall and feeder streams dispersed throughout the region. With the help of international support, it was able to make use of its natural resources to foster economic development. The North, in contrast, is less fertile and more densely populated. Though the Nile River passes through the North, it does not enjoy the same access as the South.[167]

In 1959, the central government in Khartoum signed the Nile Waters Agreement with Egypt without the input of South Sudan. The agreement included the construction of the

---

166 Ibid.
167 Cascão, *Resource-Based Conflict*, 145-149.

Jonglei Canal, which would drain wetlands in South Sudan to irrigate agricultural lands in the North and Egypt. Even at the time, severe negative impacts on the livelihoods of the South Sudanese as a result of the project were clear. Massive pastoralist communities would have to resettle, and fragile ecological systems would be disrupted. Despite the concerns raised, construction began in 1978. The communities most impacted by the Jonglei Canal were the very ones that spearheaded the guerrilla movements that would eventually lead to the Second Sudanese Civil War in the 1980s.[168]

Today, quarreling over water access between non-Arab Muslim ethnic groups and Arab pastoralist communities in the western Sudanese region of Darfur has fueled an ongoing genocide that started seventeen years ago. This particular war has been called the "the first climate change conflict" due to the aggravating effects rising temperatures and environmental degradation have had on the region. Of course, the true roots of violent conflict are incredibly complicated, influenced by overlapping disputes of ethnicity, religion, politics, and identity, but the ever-resurfacing role played by water insecurity cannot be ignored.[169]

What's interesting is South Sudan doesn't necessarily suffer from an absolute lack of water resources. It sits at the confluence of the White and Blue Niles and has access to three transboundary aquifers. According to the nation's water authority, there is more than enough water to service the needs of the population's eleven million people. Rather, the

---

168 Ibid.
169 Sova, "The First Climate Change Conflict."

water crisis experienced by South Sudan is one of distribution, management, and access. Water is economically scarce, not physically. Again, the situation is very much a problem of inadequate infrastructure.[170]

For one, South Sudan has no storage facilities to collect its water. The water pumps that do exist are few and far between, and extracting the water is exhausting and sometimes futile.[171]

"The water levels are too low so it's hard to pump—it can take an hour to fill a single jerry can," said Nachunalan, a woman from Manyabol, a village even more remote than Gumuruq.[172]

The last time pipe infrastructure was installed in the capital city of Juba was in 1937 and is currently capable of serving just 17 percent of the city's population. Few permanent facilities for water treatment exist, so chlorine and alum for single-use treatment is imported from Uganda at prohibitively high prices.[173] Still, the shortages of clean water and sanitation leave millions resorting to using fetid water collected from rivers and streams, putting them at high risk for water-borne diseases like cholera.[174]

Access to clean water may precipitate instances of conflict, but the reverse is also true. Water-related infrastructure is

---

170 Trew, "South Sudan."
171 Ibid.
172 Ibid.
173 Glinski, "Price of Water."
174 USAID, "Water."

critical to the healthy functioning of any community, making it a common target for violence and destruction. Boreholes and water pumps have been deliberately destroyed in the wake of civil wars and ongoing tensions between rivalrous groups. Displaced residents are forced to migrate away from the fighting, putting pressure on the water resources wherever they move, inevitably leading to even more displacement. As much as the water crisis has contributed to the wars in Sudan, the conflicts themselves are making the water crisis ever more intractable.

WATER WARS

Unfortunately, the complex, reciprocal relationship between water and conflict isn't unique to Sudan. It's a dangerous phenomenon playing out all across the Middle East and North Africa (MENA), the most water-stressed region in the world. In 2015, the foremost experts and leaders from MENA countries were asked by the World Economic Forum, "For which global risks is your region least prepared?" The majority response was water crises, more concerning than both political instability and unemployment.[175]

Over 60 percent of the population across the MENA region lives in areas of high surface water stress, compared with the global average of 35 percent. Reservoirs of water are being depleted at unsustainable rates, degrading natural ecosystems and aquifers. The problem is not merely related to drought and arid environments. The threat of water insecurity is multiplied by the effects of climate change, rapid

---

175 World Economic Forum, *Global Risks*.

economic growth, population growth, and urbanization. Again, much of the struggle concerns infrastructure and the way water is managed. [176]

As stated in the 2018 United Nations-World Bank report *Pathways for Peace*, "Often, it is not the scarcity of water that leads to tensions, but the way in which it is governed and administered. Inefficient use and management of water, outdated infrastructure, and inappropriate legal, political, and economic frameworks all exacerbate tensions arising from the scarcity of water."[177]

Eighty-two percent of wastewater in the Middle East and North Africa is not recycled. This is largely due to the lack of treatment facilities and sewage systems able to sustainably reintroduce water back into natural cycles. Egypt, Jordan, and Tunisia have developed methods to collect and treat wastewater but have been unable to reuse this water at any significant scale. The inability to recycle water represents a massive, missed opportunity to meet growing water demands in the region. [178]

Total water productivity, the economic returns per unit of water withdrawn, is low in the MENA region - about half the global average.[179] The food supply chain is particularly wasteful of freshwater resources, with losses occurring at each of the agricultural, processing, distribution, and consumption stages. The inefficiency of water use isn't simply a

---

176 World Bank, *Beyond Scarcity*, 1.
177 United Nations; World Bank, *Pathways for Peace*, 153.
178 World Bank, *Beyond Scarcity*, 65.
179 World Bank, *Beyond Scarcity*, 51-53.

problem of infrastructure. High subsidies are common and can mask the severity of water scarcity for those that receive them. Despite the shortages, the region has the lowest water tariffs (the price you pay a utility for water) in the world and spends the highest proportion of GDP on water subsidies. Few incentives exist to conserve water, encouraging a perpetual cycle of overuse. After all, what use is there in saving water if the government won't penalize you for wasting it and will actually pay you to use it? [180]

Like in Sudan and South Sudan, water insecurity in MENA nations is fueling both internal and external tensions. Internal conflicts over water can take place at several different levels: between pastoral communities over shared water points, between farmers over access to irrigation, and between citizens and national governments over the displacement effects of dams and hydropower plants. Water can be the nexus of group-based grievances and feelings of inequality based on which groups get access to water. These grievances are often the very ones that escalate into internal strife and full-blown violence. Across international borders, disputes can arise between countries straddling transboundary water resources.[181]

In Yemen, a country once known for its rich agricultural systems, the over-drilling of tube wells has created a devastating water crisis, one that has contributed to the ongoing civil war between the Houthi movement and the government, backed by Saudi Arabia and the United Arab Emirates

---

180 Kochhar et al., *Glass Half Empty*.
181 United Nations; World Bank, *Pathways for Peace*, 153-154.

(UAE). Since the 1970s, the extraction of the nation's groundwater has been unchecked and unregulated. The exponential increase in wells was intended to support the irrigation of farmland, but the practice has quickly become unsustainable. In 2010, the International Development Research Centre estimated withdrawals of groundwater exceeded renewal by 30 percent.[182] Over the past two decades, the total amount of renewable water resources per capita in Yemen has declined drastically. Every year, average groundwater levels drop by six meters in the regions surrounding the cities of Sana'a, Taiz, Dhamar, Amran and Sa'ada. Poorly constructed and swiftly depreciating pipe and dam infrastructure is causing sewage run-off to contaminate what little groundwater still remains.[183]

"Yemen has literally been pumping itself dry," said Daniel Varisco, an anthropologist who has worked on water-related issues in Yemen for over four decades.[184]

The fight for control over water resources has been central to the military strategies of both sides of the Yemeni civil war, and the resulting shortages have caused internal instability among the civilian population. In 2013, Al-Thawra, a large state-led newspaper at the time, stated that 70 to 80 percent of conflicts started in rural areas of Yemen were related to water.[185] From 2015 to 2017, the widespread destruction of water infrastructure led to a cholera outbreak that was called the "largest and fastest spreading outbreak of the disease

---

182 World Bank, *Republic of Yemen*, 78.
183 World Bank, "Future Impact."
184 Varisco, "Pumping Yemen Dry," 323.
185 Heffez, "Yemen Chewed."

in modern history."[186] The province of Ibb, previously the wettest region in the Arabian Peninsula, has become dry and desolate due to the influx of over two million internally displaced persons. The decline in crop yield following this catastrophic environmental transformation has left even more people starving.[187]

The list of countries similarly affected goes on and on. In Israel-Palestine, water rights are one of the core issues underlying the notoriously intractable conflict. Eighty percent of water reserves in the West Bank are controlled by Israel. At least a third of the water that Palestine does have access to is lost to aging infrastructure and leakages, yet Palestinians are systematically denied the ability to build new pipelines, water treatment centers, and desalination plants. In Gaza, the Coastal Aquifer on which the entire population depends will soon be exhausted or become contaminated by seawater. Already, 90 to 95 percent of water has become unfit for human consumption by WHO standards.[188]

For the better part of the last decade, tensions have sparked between Egypt and Ethiopia over the construction of the Great Ethiopian Renaissance Dam (GERD). The project, which is still ongoing, would divert a greater share of the Nile River to Ethiopia. Water flow to Egypt, which relies on the Nile for 85 percent of its water resources, could drop by 25 percent if the dam is filled to capacity.[189] Like many of its neighbors, Egypt has already been suffering from water

---

186 Whitehead, "Water Scarcity in Yemen."
187 Atkin, "Suffering in Yemen."
188 Lazarou, "Water in the Israel-Palestine Conflict."
189 Baconi, "Testing the Water."

scarcity due to inefficient infrastructure, cost-bearing subsidies, and deteriorating water quality. The country's irrigation and drainage infrastructure operate at only 50 percent efficiency and 40 percent cost recovery. Just half of the population is connected to piped sewage systems with wastewater treatment, and untreated sewage is causing the decline of freshwater availability.[190]

Now, the GERD is introducing stress in foreign relations to the already-fragile domestic water situation, and the two countries have nearly come to blows. For Ethiopia, the completed dam could generate up to 6,450 megawatts of cheap energy.[191] It would be the largest dam in Africa and could unlock serious economic growth for the country. Egypt, meanwhile, has been adamant that the project would damage its own water supply and has pressured its neighbors to halt construction.

In June of 2013, a leaked conversation between then Egyptian President Mohammad Morsi and top lawmakers showed them discussing military action including funding rebel groups as a means to sabotage the project. Since then, several attempts to negotiate agreements between the two countries have stalled out or ended in stalemate.[192]

In October of 2019, Ethiopian Prime Minister Abiy Ahmed issued a public statement on threats of force from Egypt. "It should be underlined that no force could stop Ethiopia from

---

190 World Bank, *Beyond Scarcity*.
191 Raphelson, "War over Water."
192 ABC, "Egyptian Politicians."

building a dam," he said. "If there is a need to go to war, we could get millions readied."[193]

Though crises related to water are presently concentrated in the Middle East and North Africa region, they may not be for long. As the global population continues to rise and climate change continues to eat away at natural resources, more and more countries will find themselves in similar situations. Countries beyond just the arid regions of the world will be at risk of water scarcity and the related political, economic, and security issues that come with it.

The complexities of the relationships presently described between water and conflict illustrate an important aspect of infrastructure. Infrastructure cannot be merely understood as individual, isolated physical assets that provide tangible services to the public. Rather, infrastructure must be understood in context of the political, economic, social, and environmental systems it interacts with. Any of the experiences of the aforementioned countries should easily explain why.

An infrastructure project may bring growth and prosperity to an underdeveloped group while simultaneously sparking feelings of injustice and damaging the home environment of another group. If managed poorly or distributed unequally, building more infrastructure can exacerbate existing tensions or even ignite new ones. This concerns the level of knowledge and experience of the institutions surrounding infrastructure. Understanding the multifaceted web of

---

193 Aljazeera, "Ethiopia's Abiy Ahmed."

influence infrastructure has will be a critical part of utilizing it in any development or peace-building process.

INFRASTRUCTURE, CONFLICT, AND PEACEBUILDING
Fragility and conflict are not always associated with water. Across the globe, billions of people live in countries plagued by violence, social and political unrest, and weak institutions unable to administer justice and peace. We have already discussed a few of the most severe situations, but many more exist. The World Bank predicts that by 2030, up to two-thirds of the world's extremely poor could come from fragile and conflict-affected states.[194] It is in these places where humanitarian needs are most intense and development goals are most difficult to achieve. Famine, displacement, and gender inequality tend to appear wherever conflict and violence exist.

Prior to the COVID-19 pandemic, violent conflict was already on the rise. According to the OECD, "In 2016, more countries experienced some form of violent conflict than at any time in the past thirty years. Close to 26,000 people died from terrorist attacks and 560,000 people lost their lives because of violence. The number of displaced people in the world is the highest since the end of the Second World War."[195]

With the pandemic and recession fueling poverty, inequality, and political unrest, countries are facing even greater risk of conflict and violence. Up to twenty-seven million people are projected to be pushed into poverty in these countries.

---

194 Corral, *Front Lines*, 18.
195 OECD, *States of Fragility 2018*, 3.

Understanding this kind of fragility and ways to mitigate it is now more important than ever.[196]

As we have already seen with water insecurity, one of those ways involves infrastructure. Interventions to prevent violence and conflict are multifaceted and politically charged. Of course, they do not come down to just infrastructure. The effects of infrastructure on peace are also not obvious. Sure, better access to water or energy might be good for people, but what can that do to stop two groups who hate each other from fighting? Nevertheless, infrastructure as a part of the peace-building process remains underutilized and its potential in shaping the security context of a country is worth investigating.

Historically, official development assistance (ODA) from advanced countries has been the primary means of addressing the needs of fragile and conflict-affected states. In 2018, $76 billion was provided to these contexts, 11.5 times the level of foreign direct investment (FDI) and 2.5 times the level of remittances.[197] The problem is this aid has primarily been short-term and humanitarian in nature. Half of all official development assistance to countries with extremely fragile contexts goes toward addressing their immediate needs for things like food, water, and shelter. Although this is undeniably important, short-term humanitarian assistance does very little to build the kind of long-term resilience that will help countries sustainably provide for themselves.

---

196 World Bank, "Fragility, Conflict & Violence."
197 OECD, *States of Fragility 2020*.

Part of effectively addressing violence is the prevention of future violence. Doing so requires allocating greater resources to the underlying issues precipitating violence. That means trying to solve the root causes of conflict rather than merely alleviating its symptoms, even if conflict is still ongoing. Lack of public services, for example, is a problem that contributes to inequality and group disenfranchisement. The deterioration in quality of services and the failure of assets that result in frequent power outages or unreliable water can lead to feelings of distrust against state institutions or international actors. Infrastructure can be an important part of a country's strategy toward improving social progress, building civilian confidence in public systems, and providing equitable opportunities for its citizens in the long term.

The success of such strategies, however, is conditional on a deep understanding of how communities are affected. Because conflicts are constantly evolving and changing, the role that infrastructure plays can shift depending on the exact context. Before conflict begins, infrastructure should be focused on building prosperous foundations for people's livelihoods in order to minimize the likelihood of tensions into violence. If conflict has already begun, it can help provide emergency services and facilitate effective responses. After conflict has stopped, it can be an important tool for rebuilding stability and providing much-needed jobs and opportunities. The following sections will discuss in detail how infrastructure has historically promoted or hindered the peace-building process across these three stages of conflict.

BEFORE THE FIGHTING BEGINS

Countries can be in states of fragility without suffering from any sort of violence. However, factors like widespread poverty, inequality, and the absence of rule of law can put these countries at much higher risk of conflict escalation. Disparities in resource allocation can ignite new center-periphery tensions based on who gets access and who doesn't. They can also aggravate existing frictions rooted in the historical exclusion of certain groups. Given how essential basic services for drinking water and energy are, infrastructure often sits at the heart of these kinds of group-based grievances. Combined with weak governance institutions lacking the capabilities to resolve disputes, these situations can quickly transform into larger, more devastating wars.

Investing in infrastructure can also be an investment in the reduction of violence and its associated costs. Unfortunately, the importance of prevention efforts is not well understood by state administrations and international actors who believe improvements in infrastructure to be far too costly and not worth the trouble. Hence, the overwhelming preference is to focus only on meeting immediate needs. This point of view isn't necessarily incorrect. For example, in Northern Mali, low population density has made infrastructure development incredibly difficult. Many populations live in physically remote areas that are hard to reach from a service provision standpoint. The gap in infrastructure led these groups to feel marginalized and abandoned by the state, further fueling the ongoing war between the northern and southern parts of Mali.[198]

---

198 Wee et al., *State Legitimacy*.

Infrastructure *is* expensive, and money may very well be better spent on a tangible impact in the present. But as costly as it may be, dealing with war is even more costly. New estimates from the World Bank and the United Nations in 2018 showed efforts focused on prevention can be incredibly effective. By eliminating the future need to expend resources on military interventions, aid, and peacekeeping, countries can actually generate savings ranging from five to sixty-nine billion dollars. In the long-term, investing in infrastructure may prove to be the financially responsible decision.[199]

Some types of infrastructure can have direct impacts beyond improving long-term development outcomes. The expansion of electricity through streetlights can deter violent acts for the simple reason that more crimes are committed in the dark. Road networks and waterways can facilitate law enforcement by providing access to communities affected by crimes. Social infrastructure like police stations, courthouses, and other government buildings directly contributes to rule of law and the quality of justice systems.[200]

WHILE THE BATTLE RAGES ON

Developing infrastructure while war is ongoing is complicated by parties to the conflict who may target it for strategic purposes. Without the right precautions, infrastructure can become an axis for power struggles that can magnify disputes. For example, during an armed conflict with the government of the Democratic Republic of the Congo, the

---

199 United Nations; World Bank, *Pathways for Peace*, 289.
200 UNOPS, *Infrastructure for Peacebuilding*, 18.

Alliance of Patriots for a Free and Sovereign Congo, a rebel militia, actively blocked the rehabilitation of a bridge in an effort to prevent the state's deployment of troops.[201]

Some programs that have experimented with infrastructure as an avenue for peacebuilding have been met with limited success. These failed attempts illustrate the relative inefficacy of infrastructure in a vacuum. At the end of the day, if institutions are weak and unstable, adding infrastructure to their list of responsibilities does little to improve outcomes.

In 2003, the United States Agency for International Development (USAID) established a program to implement "Quick Impact Projects" (QIP), which were short-term infrastructure projects designed to encourage stabilization in the country. Several issues impeded the success of QIPs and caused them to escalate rather than alleviate tensions in many Afghan provinces.[202]

The projects had the secondary objective of winning the consent of local communities to make them more receptive to state and international interventions. It was about sending a message of stability and trust in the foreign soldiers patrolling their country. True to their name, the QIPs were rushed to completion without appropriate planning for how the infrastructure would perform in the long term. Errors in the preparation phase and substandard implementation resulted in faulty projects that burdened Afghanistan with high operation and maintenance costs. When assets

---

201 United Nations Security Council, *Final Report*, 66.
202 USAID, "Quick Impact Projects."

eventually broke down and services were cut off, the surrounding populations were left with nothing but heightened tensions and greater insecurity.[203]

The desire for swift implementation required the international military to undertake the construction of schools and clinics. This undermined the ability of local Afghan institutions to deliver their own projects and left little room for community participation.[204] The people the QIPs were meant to serve weren't involved in their planning, construction, or operation. International actors presumed to know exactly the effects the projects would have. They neglected to investigate how the projects might alter local power dynamics, encourage corruption, or exacerbate regional disparities, details that could only have been found through community consultation. This lack of local ownership ultimately contributed to the strategy's failure.[205]

The logic here should have been straightforward. Who would know more about a town or village than the people of that town or village itself? The failures of the QIP program illustrate how infrastructure-based strategies for peacebuilding have historically been too focused on the physical asset itself without taking into account the broader social and economic system behind it. This has hindered the potential for infrastructure to achieve the kind of long-term development outcomes that might actually have a profound impact on peace.

---

203 UNOPS, *Infrastructure for Peacebuilding*, 23.
204 Ward, "Slow Progress in Afghanistan."
205 Jones and Howarth, *Supporting Infrastructure Development*, 33-35.

Still, effective responses to conflict, even those focused on short-term humanitarian needs, are heavily dependent on effective infrastructure. Healthcare facilities cannot function without energy capacity and water for sanitation purposes. Equipping hospital and medical care workers with the tools they need to treat patients can help prevent disease outbreaks from becoming endemic. Roads, bridges, and ports enable aid providers to reach remote communities and deliver emergency food and shelter. Telecommunications infrastructure allows states to coordinate with international aid agencies and non-governmental organizations.

In Yemen, the ongoing conflict has exacted significant tolls on the country's energy grid. Prior to the start of the civil war in 2014, two-thirds of the population had some access to electricity. In just two years, the access rate dropped to below 10 percent. In 2018, the World Bank's International Development Association (IDA) and the United Nations Office for Project Services began a project to harness Yemen's abundant supply of sunlight through a fifty-million-dollar solar power project. Termed the Yemen Emergency Electricity Access Project, the project's goal was to provide electricity to 200,000 Yemeni households, 400 healthcare facilities, and 800 schools. Today, buildings like the Al-Salam Hospital in Luhj can provide urgent care services around the clock without worrying about power outages. By involving private sector partners in the supply and installation of solar power equipment, the project was also able to generate employment opportunities and strengthen the local economy.[206]

---

206 UNOPS, "Solar Project."

The key for future interventions will be to take a multidimensional, holistic approach toward infrastructure. The long-term sustainably of assets cannot be sacrificed for a quick turnaround. That means taking the necessary time during planning and preparation stages to make sure projects are being implemented with the highest standards. It also means involving the voices and efforts of the actual communities who will receive the infrastructure services. Anything less could easily lead to even more conflict-driven fragility.

BUILDING BACK BETTER

The most significant impact infrastructure can have on the peace process likely comes after the conflict ends. In the arid regions of Northern Darfur, Sudan, water-related projects have helped displaced communities return to their homelands. Some pastoralist communities and herding groups who once fought over precious natural resources have come to collaborate on projects for their shared prosperity.[207]

As mentioned before, climate change and water scarcity have fueled much of the crisis in Darfur. Since the outbreak of war almost two decades ago, the Sahara Desert has advanced southward into Northern Sudan by about a mile a year. This has caused a severe decrease in rainfall and created an existential problem for many of the rural farming communities in the region. Crop yields have plummeted, eliminating the only source of livelihood for millions of people, and competition over water has pitted groups against each another.[208]

---

207 Carrington, "First Climate Change War."
208 Borger, "Darfur Conflict."

In 2007, the secretary general of the UN at the time called the conflict "an ecological crisis" and encouraged the international community to look past the "conventional military and political shorthand" version of the situation.[209]

Though the broader war is still ongoing, some level of peace has started to emerge in rural areas. This progress has been driven by community-led weir projects installed in a river that flows through El Fasher, Darfur's capital. Weirs are low barriers built across rivers that help control the flow of water. They've allowed more of the river to water the surrounding lands throughout the year. As a result, more farmers have been able to plant their crops. Instead of being driven away by climate change, they can stay and earn a living.[210]

More importantly, different communities have been brought together to plan and build the weirs. Groups that were once killing each other started working with each other to transform Darfur into a more prosperous region.

Atila Uras runs the United Nations Environment Programme (UNEP) in Sudan. "Everyone agrees there is a problem with the environment, with water by far the biggest priority," he told the *Guardian* in 2019.[211]

With everyone united behind this shared objective, years of hatred have finally started to dissipate. Nomadic herders invited the local farmers to a wedding in September of 2019,

---

209 Ibid.
210 Carrington, "First Climate Change War."
211 Ibid.

an event signaling real breakthrough in the quest to rebuild relations and sustain long-term peace.[212]

The improvements started by the weir projects are small relative to the challenge that still exists in Darfur, but they showcase the potential for infrastructure to serve as an axis of rebuilding. As infrastructure continues to improve, communities will be even more resilient to future shocks. Successful projects can bring cash inflows and generate jobs for the unemployed. More opportunities will arise for institutions to build capacity and ensure high-quality, sustainable service provision. Infrastructure can open up the opportunity for communities to work together toward common goals and shared prosperity.

The development experience in fragile and conflict-affected countries illustrates just how complex infrastructure is. Closing the infrastructure gap won't be as easy as finding ways to pay for more construction, although that in itself isn't by any means easy. Ensuring the resilience, sustainability, and success of infrastructure will require much more. The various tendrils of influence infrastructure has on society, the economy, and the environment will have to be examined on a project-by-project basis. Only then can closing the global infrastructure gap achieve its true potential.

---

212 Ibid.

6

DELIVERING INFRASTRUCTURE TO THE WORLD

WHERE DOES INFRASTRUCTURE SPENDING COME FROM?

Before we begin to discuss how countries can close the infrastructure gap, it will be important to discuss where infrastructure investment actually comes from. The most prominent means of financing for both developing and advanced economies is public expenditure. Governments across the world at multiple levels allocate a portion of their budgets to building and operating infrastructure projects. Odds are the roads you drive on were paid for by the state or municipality you live in. The same goes for the pipe infrastructure that brings you running water. Because of the economic necessity and broad public externalities associated with these assets, they naturally fall under the responsibility of public institutions. This kind of spending is referred to as traditional infrastructure investment.

The life cycle of any infrastructure asset can be broken down into several stages: planning, building, operating, and maintaining. Different sources of public revenue can account for each stage. Planning and building comprise the largest upfront investment. Unsurprisingly, constructing a large functioning physical structure like a highway is very expensive. Governments often use debt financing, which is revenue raised from issuing bonds, to pay for this phase of infrastructure development. They can also use revenue raised from taxing the population. Though it varies from government to government, the money used to pay for the ongoing operation and maintenance of infrastructures often comes from fees paid by users. Every time you pay your water or electricity bill, you are contributing to the continued functioning of infrastructure.

Private entities also provide investment for infrastructure projects, usually following a corporate structure. The revenues private companies generate from customers and reinvest into fixed capital assets is also considered infrastructure investment. Like governments, corporations can also issue bonds to cover the cost of the upfront investment. Typically, the sectors covered by corporations are energy and telecommunications, though this is not always the case. In the United States, roughly three-quarters of electricity customers are served by commercialized utilities like Pacific Gas and Electric (PG&E).[213] The Nashville Electric Service and the Tennessee Valley Authority it purchases power from, however, are both publicly owned and managed.[214]

---

213 US Energy Information Administration, "Investor-owned Utilities."
214 Tennessee Valley Authority, "About TVA."

Another source of private financing for infrastructure comes from institutional investors. Asset owners like pension funds, sovereign wealth funds, and insurance companies pool together the savings of many separate individuals and entities and allocate it to various income-generating or appreciating assets. The individual investors receive a return on their savings and pay a fee to the institution for its investment services. Historically these institutions have had low participation in infrastructure, but an increasing amount of interest has been expressed in recent years. For example, in 2019, the Canada Pension Plan Investment Board purchased an equity stake in the Cipoko-Palimanan Toll Road in Indonesia.[215] This specific type of investor represents a unique opportunity to close the infrastructure gap in developing countries and will be discussed in much greater detail throughout the rest of this book.

Finally, developing countries receive support from donors, foreign aid agencies, and development finance institutions for their infrastructure needs. These institutions can provide financing and assistance for low- and middle-income nations where no other alternatives exist. The multilateral development banks (MDB) are a critical part of this system. MDBs are organizations established by multiple nations to support the economic development of poorer nations. In addition to being the leading sources on development expertise, much of which has already been referenced in this book, these institutions can lend directly to developing countries for infrastructure projects. Their revenue is provided by capital subscriptions from member countries and from raising

---

215 CPP Investment Board, "Cipali Toll Road."

money in the capital markets. Among the largest MDBs are the World Bank (WB), the Asian Development Bank (ADB), the African Development Bank (AFDB), and the Inter-American Development Bank (IADB).[216]

The exact distribution of infrastructure investments from each of these sources is difficult to quantify. Different studies have offered different estimates, but general trends are clear. Private and aid-based spending is historically low compared to public spending. Using national account data for fixed capital accumulation, in conjunction with the World Bank's Private Participation in Infrastructure database, Marianne Fay et al. estimated the share of private infrastructure investment in low and middle-income countries to be somewhere between 9 to 13 percent of total investment.[217] Other studies have arrived at larger proportions, but none show levels comparable to the public sector.[218] Further, a 2019 UN report showed private investments in infrastructure have been declining in developing countries since 2012.[219] Development financing from foreign aid and the MDBs is even lower at around 5 to 8 percent of total spending.[220] The important thing to note is the historically dominant role played by public institutions with regards to infrastructure investment.

---

216 Congressional Research Service, "Multilateral Development Banks."
217 Fay et al., *Hitting the Trillion Mark*.
218 Bhattacharya, Romani, and Stern, *Infrastructure for Development*, 17.
219 United Nations, Inter-agency Task Force on Financing for Development, *Financing for Development*, 61.
220 Bhattacharya, Romani, and Stern, *Infrastructure for Development*, 17.

AN IMPOSSIBLE TASK

Closing the infrastructure gap has long been heralded as an impossible task, and for good reason. As frightening as climate change, violent conflicts, and global pandemics may be, developing countries face an incredibly steep uphill battle when it comes to building resilience through infrastructure. How are these countries, which by definition have low income, supposed to come up with the trillions of additional infrastructure spending they supposedly need? The hard truth is there is simply not enough money in these places to build the kind of energy, water, transportation, and telecommunications assets necessary to promote growth and achieve the Sustainable Development Goals.

Governments that cannot source the savings necessary to invest in public infrastructure and other development necessities fall into something development economists refer to as a "fiscal trap."[221] Growth and development are conditional on these investments, but governments of impoverished nations are too cash-strapped and indebted to finance them. The absence of roads, energy, and health infrastructure reinforce cycles of poverty and prohibit the private sector from flourishing. Poverty leads to low public investment which then leads to more poverty, creating a viscous cycle many countries struggle to get out of.

After the collapse of the US housing bubble and the great financial crisis of the late 2000s, many governments faced severely constrainend fiscal space. To survive the recession, governments were forced to dig deep into their budgets to

---

221 Sachs, *Common Wealth*, 425.

support faltering industries and support their economies. This caused public debt to skyrocket, limiting the amount governments could borrow and spend. As debt loads continued to rise, countries felt the need for fiscal consolidation. They needed to reduce deficit spending in order to achieve macroeconomic stability. This was especially true for the governments of developing countries, many of which never had strong financial stability to begin with. In short, because of the inexplicable and irresponsibly risky behavior of Wall Street banks, the poorest parts of the world lost the ability to spend money.[222]

As the full blow of the COVID-19 pandemic and economic crisis has begun to unfold, the problem has become exponentially worse. Entire industries have come to a full stop, many of which emerging economies dependent on—tourism, being just one example. With millions of people losing their jobs and sliding back into poverty, countries are under extreme pressure to provide direct income and medical support for the unemployed. Doing so has forced them to borrow even more heavily, forcing them to take on unsustainable levels of debt.

With public budgets stretched as thin as they are, the outlook for a global infrastructure development agenda is bleak. Unless there are significant shifts in the sources of investment, fiscal traps cannot be escaped, and the infrastructure gap will not be closed. The public sector simply does not have the money to spend, and, unfortunately, countries are unlikely to come across trillions of dollars hiding away

---

[222] Inderst and Stewart, *Institutional Investment*, 4-5.

somewhere in a treasure chest. Where else can countries look for their infrastructure financing needs?

Most of the money for infrastructure developing countries cannot raise themselves comes from the aid agencies we've already mentioned. The solar power project powering the Al-Salam Hospital in Yemen was paid for by a grant from the International Development Association, the World Bank's fund for the poorest countries in the world.[223] This kind of money usually take the form of direct aid or concessional loans, which carries below-market interest rates and have generous terms. The important thing to know is that this money is not necessarily *invested*. Occasionally, successful projects do allow the MDBs to generate a return, but the purpose is to provide assistance, not to make a profit. Although conditions are attached to grants and loans, as long as the positive development outcomes are achieved, that money has fulfilled its purpose.

Aid might sound like the right idea when it comes to these types of issues. It sounds the most moral. After all, if the poor are in such desperate need of infrastructure, wouldn't it be good for the rich to offer more of their money to build it? Truth is, there isn't a lot of money in the world that's willing to be given away like that, nor should such exorbitant sums be given away. Yes, the Yemeni solar project undoubtedly had a massive impact on many lives and every project similar to it goes an equally long way. But the scale of the problem is much, much greater. In 2020, the World Bank Group disbursed a total of fifty-four billion dollars to developing

---

223 UNOPS, "Solar Project."

countries.[224] That sounds like a lot of money (and it is), but it's a billion-dollar solution to a trillion-dollar problem, and only a portion of it goes toward infrastructure. The rest of it is earmarked for other development needs like health, education, private sector growth, and poverty reduction, all of which are just as important as infrastructure.

Charities also tend to stay away from spending on infrastructure, which are inherently long-term assets. It takes years and years to design, build, and operate infrastructure in a way that's economically and socially viable. The integration of infrastructure into a society is also highly regulated by both national and regional laws. Paying for the development of a new wastewater treatment center in Sudan, for example, isn't quite the same as delivering cases of bottled water to poor rural communities. The former may be the more sustainable and long-term solution, but it's way more expensive and the benefits will only manifest long into the future. Charitable funds want to know their donations are making an impact. The last thing they want is to take a gamble on a long-term project that may or may not pan out. Though many are quite sizable, only a select few group of donors choose to participate in infrastructure. It's simply too complicated and not worth the effort.

It's really no wonder why infrastructure is underfunded in poor countries. National income isn't high enough for governments to raise taxes and fund it publicly. Borrowing domestically isn't much of an option for the same reason. Borrowing internationally is constrained by the fear of deficit

---

224 World Bank, *Unprecedented Times*, 13.

spending and potential debt crises that inevitably become a tax burden on already impoverished populations. MDBs and governments of developed nations do their best to provide technical and financing assistance where they can, but the amount of money they can provide is small relative to the level of investment needed. So where will the money come from? Are the poorest parts of the world just doomed to make do with the meager stock of infrastructure they have now?

WHERE'S ALL THE MONEY IN THE WORLD?

So far, we have referred to infrastructure as a physical asset and investments in infrastructure as having socioeconomic returns. If countries spend more money on infrastructure, they will be more resilient in their fight against poverty and climate change. Now, we will explore infrastructure's unique dual role as a *financial* asset and investment in infrastructure as having *financial* returns. It is this aspect of infrastructure that may unlock the trillions of dollars needed to close the gap.

Every investment has to have the potential for some kind of return. Otherwise, it isn't an investment. Financial investments have financial returns. Stocks, for example, provide investors with partial ownership of a public company. If the company does well, the stock's value appreciates, and the investor can sell it for more than she bought it for. Some stocks also pay out dividends directly to their shareholders. Bonds are debt investments that pay fixed interest payments over the bond's duration.

Physical objects can also be financial assets. Real estate, for example, is both a form of investment and a functional product. If you buy an apartment in a booming metropolitan city, you can earn cash flows by renting it out or by selling it for a higher price. Gold, silver, and other precious metals are other examples of what we call real assets. Depending on a particular investor's preferences, any combination of financial assets can make up a portfolio of investments.

Certain types of financial assets play a role beyond allowing investors to make more money. They can be important financing tools for their issuers to accomplish various goals. For example, the United States Department of the Treasury sells bonds in what are called the capital markets to finance the government's spending. Taxation, the government's primary source of revenue, often isn't timely enough to match exact spending needs. To make up the difference, the government borrows money upfront and repays its debt over time. Investors who purchase the bonds are essentially loaning the government money in exchange for money promised in the future.

The dual role the bond plays for both parties to the transaction makes it something called a financial instrument. The importance of this system cannot be overstated. Without the ability to issue bonds, the government's operations would be severely inhibited. The trillions of dollars of stimulus passed during the pandemic would never have happened. The same system, including equities, is used by corporations.

By incentivizing regular citizens to channel their savings into these financial assets, a country can flourish and grow.[225]

Financial instruments vary in how effective they are in fulfilling the dual goals of the givers and receivers of capital. The most reliable instruments are the most widely used. Stocks and bonds, for example, are two types of investments that have historically dominated the capital markets. Over the years, they've become indispensable tools for both public and private institutions. Companies and governments need cash on hand, and investors want cash in the future. Both parties in a typical stock or bond transaction know what they are getting out of the deal. Because of this, the markets for stocks and bonds are incredibly sophisticated. They're also massive. Global equity markets are valued at around ninety-five trillion dollars.[226] Bonds markets are even larger at around $130 trillion.[227] That's about the size of the entire global economy.[228] That should give you an indication of just how much money exists out there.

NEGATIVE INTEREST RATE BONDS

All of that invested money is, well, already invested. Unfortunately, it isn't just out there floating in the ether waiting to be spent. Most of it is sitting happily, collecting interest checks or appreciating in value until a better investment comes along. But not all of it.

---

225 Green, "Financial Instrument."
226 SIFMA, *2020 Capital Markets*, 7.
227 Ibid.
228 World Bank, "Size of World Economy."

Allow me to introduce you to the world of negative interest rate bonds.

Imagine that your friend wants to buy an item of clothing he or she can't afford yet. They come to you and ask for a loan of one hundred dollars. You agree to lend them the money. In return, you might expect to receive a payment of, say, $110 dollars in a month or two. At the very least, you'd want to get your one hundred dollars back. In this situation, however, not only do you agree to lend your friend the money, but you also accept a smaller return payment of ninety dollars. In other words, you are paying your friend to use your money. That's essentially the logic behind negative interest-rate bonds.

There is way more money than you might think invested into debt instruments with negative yields. In December of 2020, the Bloomberg Barclays Global Negative Yielding Debt Index reached record high-levels of eighteen trillion dollars.[229] Let that number sink in. There is eighteen trillion dollars out there that actively sought out bonds where investors are charged rather than paid money to hold them.

For all our analysis on money that can't just be given away, it certainly seems as if purchasing negative-yielding bonds is doing just that. In reality, the reasoning behind why these bonds exist and why investors purchase them is a little more complicated. Bonds issued by national governments are typically viewed as having low risk and high liquidity. That means investors that purchase them can be confident they'll get their money back and there will always be a reliable market to sell

---

229 Mullen and Ainger, "World's Negative-Yielding Debt."

the bonds whenever necessary. The yield on the United States ten-year treasury is considered in finance to be a "risk-free rate." The stability of the US government combined with its right to tax the American population makes it reasonably certain it will always pay back its debts.[230]

During times of low economic activity or recession, investors often seek to park their cash in safe assets like government bonds out of fear of losing money in the stock market, for example. At the same time, central banks will lower interest rates to incentivize borrowing and stimulate spending. In extreme situations, monetary authorities can actually bring rates below zero and charge investors to hold their money. In 2014, the European Central Bank first cut its rates below zero as a response to low inflation. Other countries like Japan, Sweden, Denmark, and Germany have followed suit. Eighty percent of Germany's government bonds have negative yields as do all of the Danish government's bonds.[231]

You might think outright losing money would be enough reason to move money away from these bonds, but the size of the negative-yielding bond market has only risen. It's a massive, eighteen-trillion-dollar sign that investors have nothing better to invest in. If you include bonds with rates just barely above zero, that number skyrockets even further. In March of 2020, the entire US yield curve representing all US treasuries with different maturities dropped below one percent for the first time in history.[232] There may be trillions upon trillions

---

230 Kenny, "Safety."
231 Ainger, "Bonds That Eat Your Money."
232 Mohamed, "US Yield Curve."

of dollars that are already invested in the world, but a huge portion of it isn't making much return, if any at all. It's all money that would theoretically be available, given a better alternative investment.

TRILLION-DOLLAR PROBLEMS

Negative-interest rate bonds aren't even the half of it when it comes to money that can be put to better use. As large as the various investment markets are, there's even more money out there. Money that could also be mobilized if offered a decent return. According to Jim Yong Kim, ex-president of the World Bank, there is "eight trillion dollars literally sitting in the hands of rich people, under their very large mattresses."[233] That money is *literally* just sitting there, doing absolutely nothing but adorning the beautiful homes of the folks who keep it.

The world is full of trillion-dollar problems. Mountains will have to move in order for climate change, childhood stunting, extreme poverty, infectious diseases, and social inequality to be solved. Luckily for us, the world is also overflowing with trillions of dollars that, if mobilized in the right way, can move those mountains. The problem lies in somehow channeling all that money toward investing in real solutions for the world's poor. You can't ask the rich to give it away. That would never work. You also can't forcibly take it away from them. There isn't a political world order nearly strong enough to do that, to say nothing of the catastrophic consequences

---

233 Kim, "Good Life."

that would occur if it was ever attempted. But what you can do is ask them to invest it.

It's simple math. All else equal, any rate of return on an investment is preferable to a zero or negative interest rate. If you're going to invest your money anyway, you might as well invest it in something worthwhile. If given the right reasons and incentives, it's possible all that money could be coaxed out. But in order to mobilize private capital specifically toward solving the world's foremost development challenges, there would have to be something to invest in—something that improves living conditions and provides widespread positive externalities while offering a generous rate of return on investors' money. Something that can simultaneously be a productive physical asset and a financial asset...

Can you guess what that something might be?

7

A PERFECT PAIRING

MORGAN AND JAMIE

Let's imagine two friends named Morgan and Jamie are living in some random Western country. Morgan works in a lawnmower manufacturing warehouse as a day laborer on the production line. His daily tasks consist of inspecting various parts of machinery and quality-checking products. It's a difficult job and the hours are long, but it pays decently well and provides some insurance benefits. His favorite thing is coming home every day to a hot shower and a warm meal. Morgan operates on a strict budget. He always covers all his essential expenses and saves a fixed portion first before allowing some extra spending money for his family.

Let's also imagine the federal government of this random Western country has a national public pension plan for all its citizens. So, in addition to his own savings, a small percentage is taken out from all of Morgan's paychecks to contribute to his pension. One day, when he stops working, he'll receive a monthly check from the government to fund his retirement.

Finally, let's imagine this country enters a deep economic recession. Luckily, Morgan is able to keep his job, but his pay and hours are deducted significantly. He is forced to make some difficult decisions regarding how much he spends. Among other forgone luxuries, Morgan's daughter won't be able to get a new smartphone this year and the family will have to shop at cheaper stores for clothes and groceries. He'll also have to start allocating a smaller portion of his income to his personal savings. The amount Morgan spends on rent and utilities, however, will not change, even if the bills get more expensive due to the recession. At the end of the day, the lights have to stay on, and the water has to keep running. The percentage of his paycheck allocated to his pension plan also won't change because of federal law.

Jamie works in the finance industry as an investment manager. Specifically, he invests on behalf of the national pension plan, the very one he, Morgan, and all their fellow working citizens contribute to. His primary responsibility is to pool all that money into a pension fund and grow it so it can sustain itself and provide retirement income benefits for the country long into the future. To do so, Jamie and his team invest the money into various income-generating and appreciating assets like stocks and bonds. If the pension fund does not grow at, say, 4 percent per year, the system will fall apart. The pension would not be able to guarantee benefits to citizens a couple decades into the future. Either workers will have to contribute more money or retired folks will receive fewer benefits or both. None are acceptable options.

When the recession hits, Jamie is also forced to make some tough decisions. Consumer confidence and consumption are down. Several of the companies whose stocks the pension are currently invested in are underperforming, and the price of their shares are declining rapidly. One of those companies is a major technology conglomerate that sells the most popular smartphone in the market, the exact model that Morgan's daughter won't be getting this year. As a result, Jamie decides that maintaining the pension fund's position in recession-affected stocks is too risky.

Jamie's decision causes the pension fund to invest heavily in bonds, specifically investment grade corporate and government bonds. These assets are much less risky than the stocks, given the issuers credit quality and the fixed stream of income promised by holding the securities. Bondholders are also contractually paid out before shareholders. However, as a response to the recession, the central bank of the country decides to lower interest rates in order to discourage saving and stimulate borrowing and spending. The yield on the bonds purchased by the pension fund drops incredibly low, lower than they've ever been before. Finally, they reach a point where the pension fund would actually lose money by purchasing bonds and holding them to maturity. In other words, interest rates become negative.

Now Jamie is stuck between a rock and a hard place. On one hand, he doesn't want to risk losing money by investing in a tumbling stock market. On the other hand, he won't *make* any money by purchasing bonds. Either way, he has to figure out how to get that four percent return so pensioners will receive their checks ten, fifteen, and twenty-five years later. With stocks and bonds both being unfavorable at the moment, he has to find something else to invest in.

Jamie meets up with Morgan at a bar to catch up. He tells Morgan about his problems finding good investments for the pension plan to hold during the recession. Morgan sympathizes with his plight but can think of no better solution either. Morgan then shares with Jamie his personal struggles during the recession. How he wasn't making enough money to sustain his old lifestyle and how his family had to cut back on their spending. At least, he says, the lights are still turn on and hot water is still running. In a fit of inspiration, Jamie realizes what he can invest in: infrastructure.

Jamie takes a portion of the pension fund's assets and uses it to purchase the wastewater infrastructure and grid power station connected to Morgan's home. The fund takes responsibility for service provision and maintenance. To ensure its investment isn't lost to corroding pipes and other system failures, the pension fund spends a considerable amount repairing and rebuilding the infrastructure. The households receiving water and power actually benefit from improvements in efficiency. In return, the assets grow in value and provide the pension fund with long-term, stable cash flows. The return is enough to reach 4 percent, and Jamie's fiduciary responsibility to the stakeholders of the pension is honored.

THE BIGGEST ASSET OWNERS
To be clear, the above scenario is only a hypothetical. A realistic portrayal of what infrastructure investment looks like and what it can accomplish is far more complicated. But the hypothetical does illustrate the essential logic behind why infrastructure is worth looking at from a financial

standpoint. For certain types of investors, it has a number of extremely attractive attributes.

The "types" of investors I am referring to are institutional investors. The vast majority of invested capital isn't controlled by individuals like you and me but by large investment institutions. These institutions pool together the savings of many individuals and companies and invest it on their behalf. They are the largest asset owners in the world and have the power to purchase and sell investments on a scale unparalleled by any other kind of investor. It will be worthwhile to briefly describe some of these investors and their main differences.

PENSION FUNDS

One of the oldest wisdoms associated with money is saving for your retirement. Across the world, countries have developed a variety of schemes to help their citizens accumulate wealth to sustain them financially once they stop working. These schemes broadly fall under the category of pension systems. Andrew Ang, author of *Asset Management: A Systematic Approach to Factor Investing*, separates pension savings into four categories: national pension plans, private defined benefit pension plans, private defined contribution pension plans, and pension plans privately managed by individuals.[234]

The largest and most common pensions are created and run at the national level on behalf of private citizens. You may be familiar with them being referred to as social security. Under these systems, a percentage of individual paychecks is taken

---

234 Ang, *Asset Management*, 13-24.

out in the form of a payroll tax. The combined contributions of many millions of working citizens are pooled together into a fund. The fund is then grown through various investments and is drawn from to provide retirement benefits to eligible citizens. They are managed by investment professionals hired by the government.[235] National pension funds are some of the largest collections of assets in the world. The US Social Security Trust Funds, for example, house a whopping $2.9 trillion in assets. The Government Pension Investment Fund of Japan is not too far behind with $1.5 trillion in assets under management (AUM).[236]

Individual corporations and local government offices can also offer pension plans for their employees. In defined benefit plans, the employer guarantees a fixed retirement benefit based on factors like wage rate and number of years in service. For example, the California Public Employees' Retirement System pays a larger benefit to teachers retiring at age fifty-five than teachers retiring at sixty-three or older. The expenditures are drawn from a $444 billion fund invested into various assets on their behalf. [237]

These two types of pension funds have a fiduciary obligation to pay out benefits to their members. Defined contribution pension plans, in contrast, are not pooled together into single funds. Rather, the employer pays a fixed contribution to an employee's retirement bank account. However much the individual ends up with once they retire is however much they

---

235 Ibid.
236 SWFI, "100 Largest Public Pension Rankings."
237 top100funds, "California Public Employees Retirement System."

receive. The choice of investments is also left up to the individual. 401(k) retirement plans are an example of a defined contribution pension. Because these pension systems don't lead to the same kind of massive funds that can make billions of dollars' worth of investment, they will be of less interest to the rest of this chapter.[238]

SOVEREIGN WEALTH FUNDS

The 1980s was called *La Decada Perdida* in Latin America, "the Lost Decade." The continent's largest economies were crippled by debt crises and went completely bankrupt. The historical causes for "the lost decade" are quite extensive and go back to colonial times, but a key issue was a lack of liquidity. Countries did not have enough currency on hand to cover their liabilities and pay interest on the money they owed. In response, the United States and the International Monetary Fund essentially told them to save more. This led to rapid growth of sovereign wealth funds.[239]

In some countries, the excess revenues from particularly profitable industries are collected into an investment fund. Often, this happens with countries that grow rich through the export of a valuable commodity like oil. If all those riches were invested back into the oil sector these countries would risk becoming over dependent on a single sector and become more vulnerable to price shocks. Instead, the money

---

238 Ang, *Asset Management*, 13-24.
239 Ang, *Asset Management*, 4-13.

is turned into a sovereign wealth fund that invests outside of the country in diversified sectors.[240]

The exact mandates and goals of sovereign wealth funds depend on the country they originate from. In general, they represent the interests of the citizens of that country and the money can be deployed in various ways to meet those interests. Sovereign wealth funds are also used to smooth consumption and wealth across different generations of citizens. If one generation suffers from economic recession and high unemployment, it can be supported by the contributions of previous generations through the sovereign wealth fund.[241]

Like many of the world's pension funds, sovereign wealth funds are massive. The Norway Government Pension Fund, which is not really a "pension" fund because it is funded by oil revenues, is the largest sovereign wealth fund in the world with over $1.2 trillion assets. The China Investment Corporation comes in at a close second with one trillion dollars in AUM.[242]

Other types of large asset owners include university endowments, insurance companies, and private family foundations. Though not quite as large as the biggest pension funds and sovereign wealth funds, these institutions also represent a large portion of the world's financial capital. To be clear, asset *owners* are distinct from asset *managers* like private equity funds, hedge funds, and infrastructure funds. Because asset

---

240 Ibid.
241 Ibid.
242 SWFI, "Largest Sovereign Wealth Fund Rankings."

owners often lack the personnel and expertise for deal making and investment management, they often hire external managers to grow their funds. This, however, is not always the case, as asset owners are increasingly building the capacity to invest directly on their own.

A PERFECT PAIRING

Altogether, OECD researchers estimate institutional investors in just OECD and G20 countries have at least $64.8 trillion in combined AUM.[243] Including commercial banks, McKinsey estimated global institutional investment resources to be around $120 trillion.[244] When it comes to the amount of money that can truly make a dent on the infrastructure gap, it is these investors who will have to step up to the plate.

There are many different types of infrastructure and several different ways to invest in it, but, like stocks and bonds, a number of general characteristics unify infrastructure as an asset class. Fortunately, many of these characteristics align very well with the investment goals of many institutional investors. Infrastructure investments are long-term assets with long-term cash flows. Most infrastructure is built to last several decades, and infrastructure services are typically protected by long-term contracts and government regulation. Institutional investors often hold long-term liabilities and can benefit greatly from holding long-term assets. Pension funds, for example, have obligations not only to retirees in the present but also to retirees indefinitely into the future. Rather

---

243 OECD, *Green Infrastructure*.
244 Woetzel et al., *Bridging Global Infrastructure*, 17.

than investing in short-term, speculative assets, these funds benefit greatly from having their capital locked up in assets that can deliver returns over the course of many years.[245]

In general, infrastructure investments can generate yields above that of the fixed-income market. In the historically low-interest environment we are in now, institutional investors are desperate to find better options than bonds. It isn't just that higher yields would be preferable, they are needed for institutions to uphold their obligations to their stakeholders. In this regard, infrastructure represents a great alternative.[246]

The demand for infrastructure services is largely resistant to shifts in the business cycle and macroeconomic downturns. Think about the last time you had to actively decide whether or not to pay your water or electricity bill. Even in the most extreme circumstances, infrastructure assets can still generate income. This makes their cash flows stable and predictable, an attractive aspect for any investment. Infrastructure can also be resistant to inflation risk, depending on contractual arrangements around the investment. Finally, investments in these assets are generally uncorrelated with traditional asset classes, offering the opportunity for portfolio diversification.[247]

There are also a number of reasons why this pairing is advantageous from a development perspective. First and foremost

---
245 Sharma, "Emerging Asset Class."
246 Inderst and Stewart, *Institutional Investors*, 6.
247 Bagínski, "Infrastructure as an Asset Class."

is affordability. The most expensive part of any infrastructure project comes during the initial planning and construction phases. The actual operation of roads, railways, power generation, water and sanitation are comparatively less expensive than building the hard infrastructure itself. These larger expenses, also known as capital costs, are what drive up the cost of service for actual users. If project developers can amortize, or spread out, capital costs over longer periods of time, the price users pay for their infrastructure services actually decreases. This has a direct income effect on the poor. Institutional investors with long-term investment horizons could provide this kind of financing.[248]

The Global Infrastructure Facility (GIF), a partnership organization between various MDBs and national governments, ran a simulation on the effect of longer-term debt on a large power project going to market in West Africa. Using maturities and costs of capital suggested by institutional investors who became advisory partners to the GIF, it was found that consumer energy tariffs would drop nearly 20 percent. That's a significant price drop for low-income households. If implemented at scale, this strategy could have a direct effect on poverty alleviation.[249]

Second, the interest of institutional investors often aligns closely with development agendas. Because they are investing in the long term, these investors benefit safeguards and stability. In other words, they are less willing to put money into projects that will cut corners. It also means they will have less

---

248 Schwartz, "Institutional Investment in Infrastructure."
249 Ibid.

tolerance for corruption or any other regulatory hindrances to the sound functioning of infrastructure assets.[250]

Recent research has also found institutional investors with the right expertise can be great operators of infrastructure. In many cases, public users have seen similar if not improved levels of service. A 2017 PwC report analyzed the performance of UK water and energy assets following acquisition by investors. It found marked improvements in service efficiency, with annual reductions in water leakage of 13 percent and 29 percent reductions in electricity outages. These results are largely due to the new owners spending a lot more money on improving the assets. In 2014, capital expenditures on water and electric utilities grew at an average rate of 112 percent, compared to just 33 percent growth in 2004. Because of the long-term returns these funds are seeking, there is far more incentive to invest in the longevity and performance of the asset.[251]

For many of the above reasons, there has been an increasing amount of interest from institutional investors in utilizing infrastructure as an alternative asset. In a 2017 survey of large asset managers and asset owners, the Global Infrastructure Hub found 90.3 percent of institutional investors intended to increase their allocations to infrastructure within the next three to five years.[252] In 2019, there were 4,000 different institutions making such investments, a record high.[253]

---

250 Ibid.
251 PwC/GIIA, *Global Infrastructure Investment*, 11.
252 Blanc-Brude, Whittaker, and Yim, *Investor Perceptions*, 5.
253 Preqin, *Global Infrastructure Report*, 3.

In theory, even greater allocations of private capital to infrastructure are possible. Take a moment to consider what that means. Because of its potential as a financial asset, infrastructure could become a conduit for trillions of dollars' worth of development spending. It can attract money that wants to be invested in addition to money given away. It could be the single greatest channel of development assistance countries have access to.

BILLIONS TO TRILLIONS

What I am suggesting here is a significant deviation from several decades of traditional development thinking. Because of infrastructure's primary role as a public good, it has always been considered the responsibility of public institutions. Private sector involvement is not by any means a new idea, but many academics and politicians have cast doubts on the private sector's ability to provide infrastructure in a way that is ultimately beneficial to a society.

As Jeffrey Sachs, one of the most prolific development thinkers of the modern era, writes in his 2008 *New York Times* bestseller *Common Wealth: Economics for a Crowded Planet*, "If core infrastructure is left to the private market, there will tend to be under-provision, monopoly prices, and exclusion of the poor."[254]

It's understandable why Sachs was so skeptical. It isn't entirely unfair to characterize the private sector by its greed, corruption, and exploitative tendencies. Entire factions of

---

254 Sachs, *Common Wealth*, 421.

philosophical and economic thinkers attribute modern states of underdevelopment to free-market capitalism.[255] It's undeniable that global challenges related to poverty, inequality, and environmental degradation are at least somewhat rooted in globalism and other market forces. If capitalism is what created these problems in the first place, how can it possibly be a part of their solution?

At the turn of the century, world leaders gathered at The Millennium Development Summit of the United Nations to adopt a global agenda for meeting the needs of the world's poor. The result was the creation of eight Millennium Development Goals (MDGs) and a commitment from all 191 member nations to achieve them by the year 2015. Among these goals were the eradication of extreme poverty and the achievement of universal primary education.[256] Because of the fiscal trap, it was well understood that the poorest countries wouldn't be able to do it on their own. The widely accepted solution to this problem was a greater influx of foreign aid, which Sachs argued would be more than sufficient to meet the MDGs.[257]

"The UN Millennium Project demonstrated that comprehensive investments in the critical areas—agriculture, health, education, and infrastructure—if taken to scale for the poorest countries, can be covered within the international commitment of 0.7 percent of donor income as development aid. With a rich-world annual income of roughly $35 trillion,

---

255 McMichael, *Development and Social Change*.
256 Kumar, Kumar, and Vivekadhish, "Millennium Development Goals."
257 Sachs, *Common Wealth*, 470.

0.7 percent of GNP is around $245 billion per year, compared with actual aid flows of roughly one hundred billion dollars per year. The additional $145 billion per year would be sufficient to close the financing gap for the Millennium Villages, disease control, national-scale infrastructure, and much more."

Unfortunately, these estimates of the costs of financing development were horribly off. Though substantial progress had been made toward achieving the MDGs by 2015, much of it was uneven, and a number of salient challenges were ignored. World leaders realized achieving sustainable development would require far more wide-reaching action than was encompassed by the MDGs. Simply put, the task at hand was more difficult and more costly than world leaders originally imagined.

The result was the adoption of a new set of goals called the Sustainable Development Goals (SDG) and a timeline to achieve them by the year 2030. This new agenda includes seventeen goals with 169 targets, compared to the eight goals and twenty-one targets set by the MDGs. Included in this shift is a need to address the inclusiveness and equity of development so that progress isn't being concentrated both within and between countries. This is embodied in the tenth goal, to reduce inequality, and the sixteenth, to ensure peace and justice. The SDGs also place greater recognition of the scale of the climate crisis that looms in the backdrop of all other challenges. The sixth goal, clean water and sanitation, the seventh, affordable and clean energy, and the thirteenth, climate action, all have to account for drastic changes to the environment. Finally, while the MDGs focused exclusively on the needs of developing countries, the SDGs necessitate action and investment from all countries. Given the interconnectedness of our modern global community, whether through trade, communication, or most importantly, the environment, none of the greatest development challenges can be solved without the participation of the entire world.[258]

Foreign aid alone isn't enough. Official Development Assistance (ODA), an OECD measure of foreign aid, totaled $152.8 billion in 2019.[259] As we've already established, the yearly investment deficits for infrastructure alone number well into the trillions, to say nothing of financing solutions to global health challenges and violent conflict. If countries are to retrofit their infrastructure to adapt to climate change in addition to supporting socioeconomic development, a global annual investment of $6.9 trillion will be needed.[260] Though a substantial proportion of this is needed in rich countries, $152.8 trillion is still a mere fraction of what developing countries require.

Recognizing the scale of the challenges, the international development community has coined the phrase "billions to trillions," an indication of the need to source massively greater amounts of capital to finance sustainable development.[261] It represents a new paradigm that calls for channeling resources and investments from as many places as possible, both nationally and internationally. Doing so will

---

258 Kumar, Kumar, and Vivekadhish, "Millennium Development Goals."
259 OECD, "OECD and Donor Countries."
260 OECD/The World Bank/ UN Environment, *Financing Climate Futures*, 20.
261 World Bank Group, *From Billions to Trillions*.

be impossible without involving the private sector. This is not to say that foreign aid and development assistance is unimportant, nor that private sector financing can be a full replacement for aid. In fact, concessional resources will be more critical than ever to mobilize private investments and ensure its inclusiveness and sustainability. With this aid, countries can develop the institutional capacity to catalyze partnerships with the private sector and develop rigorous policy environments that can translate these partnerships into real social progress. In this way, billions of dollars of assistance can be converted into trillions of dollars of total financing, and, if all goes well, an equivalent amount of change.

TAKING A CHANCE ON CHANGE

It would be wrong of me to say this isn't a gamble. The transition to greater private provision of sustainable infrastructure is a venture into new territory. We're taking a bet that the end result will be the eradication of poverty, resilience to climate change, and recovery from conflict. It's a big bet, but the stakes are high, and time is running out. The supply of resources held by institutional investors is vast and untapped. If the right partnerships can be formed to utilize these resources, the future of sustainable development could be brighter than ever. I'm not arguing that we should hand over the reins of development to the private sector, but I am saying this opportunity can no longer be ignored.

But it isn't by any means certain. Make no mistake. The primary objective of institutional investors is to turn a profit. Social progress to them may only be a mere side effect.

There are no guarantees that the worst aspects of capitalistic approaches won't materialize. However, given the size of the challenges that lay before us, the world is in no position to take the safe route, if there even is one. We'll have to use every innovation and tool at our disposal to make this work. Consider the words of Mark Plant, COO of the Center for Global Development:[262]

"Instead, we need to bet more on new ways of doing business, new kinds of projects, new tax regimes. We need to ramp up these small experiments both in terms of size and scope. To do this, leaders must be willing to break old rules, understand that many bets won't pay off, and risk that the magic bullets will never be found. And we need to draw more players to the table, to raise the pot and the returns. But if we continue to play the same old development games, billions will never become trillions. We're running out of time if we want to make the SDGs a reality in 2030."

The world is emerging from one global crisis only to find itself on the precipice of another one. The channeling of private institutional investment into sustainable infrastructure is a path that must be seriously considered if we are to meet the Sustainable Development Goals. It's time to take a chance on change.

---

262 Center for Global Development, "Hope for Mobilizing."

8

RISKY BUSINESS

In practice, despite upward trends in interest, current institutional investment in infrastructure is actually quite low. Compared to both infrastructure needs and total assets under institutional management, it's almost insignificant. According to OECD data, institutional investors hold just $1.04 trillion worth of infrastructure assets accumulated over several decades, a meager percentage of their total AUM. Only a few pension funds, mostly from Canada and Australia, have allocations to infrastructure above 10 percent.[263]

Almost all of that $1.04 trillion is concentrated in already-existing infrastructure in developed countries. In the UK, for example, there has been a mass transfer of ownership of infrastructure from private corporations and public companies to institutional investors. Today, upwards of 56 percent of water assets, all major airports, and the majority of seaports in the UK have been acquired by pension funds from

---

263 OECD, *Green Infrastructure*.

Canada and various investment groups from Hong Kong, Australia, and London.[264]

These kinds of investments are needed to maintain and upgrade current stocks of infrastructure, but they do little to solve our problem of closing the global infrastructure gap. That would require investments in *new* infrastructure and in emerging rather than advanced economies, where needs are the highest. What exactly is stopping these institutions from allocating more of their capital to infrastructure, and why do they avoid developing countries?

A RISKY BUSINESS

In the 1990s, the city of Sydney in Australia became interested in building a tunnel that would connect the east and west sides of the central business district. It was thought the project would save travel time for people going across the city. At the time, however, a feasibility study found the tunnel to be of little economic value due to the high cost of tunneling and the low levels of traffic moving east to west across the city. In 1998, the state government of New South Wales proposed the project anyway.[265]

The tunnel was to be built, owned, and operated by a private sector party to transfer risk away from the public sector. In 2002, the project contract was awarded to a project company composed of Cheung Kong Infrastructure, a Hong Kong based investment group, and two other private equity asset

---

264 PwC/GIIA, *Global Infrastructure Investment*, 3.
265 Phibbs, "Driving Alone," 365-370.

managers. The final cost was $800 million. The government, however, was adamant it wouldn't cover any cost overruns caused by changes in design specifications or construction delays. This meant the investors would be held liable for complications in the project's development.[266]

When the tunnel opened to the public in 2005, everyone's worst fears came true. The amount of traffic going through the tunnel was dismally low, not even 50 percent of forecasted levels. The toll revenue was well below what was required to break even. Within just four months, the majority owner of the project wrote down the value of the investment by $102 million. Not enough money was being generated to cover interest payments. Two years later, the owners had no choice but to sell the tunnel at a significant loss.[267]

The Cross City Tunnel in Sydney is a great example of why private institutional investors have historically avoided infrastructure. Even in developed nations, deal making and project implementation are by no means easy. Part of that is the limited experience investors have when it comes to managing infrastructure assets and risks. If, for example, they want to reap returns on direct investments in project equity (rather than purchasing the stock of an infrastructure company), they also have to understand how to own and operate the actual assets.

As many attractive attributes as infrastructure investments have, they carry an equal number of risks. Not all investors

---

266 Ibid.
267 Ibid.

are willing to put up large, upfront investments and wait several years to generate cash flows. For projects involving the construction of new assets, delays and overruns can be very costly. If investors are held liable for these additional costs, the returns on their investments can be compromised.

There is also operating risk related to the demand for infrastructure services. For example, building a new toll road won't be very fruitful if no one wants to drive on it. The same goes for water and energy infrastructure. If demand turns out to be significantly less than estimated levels, investors might find themselves overpaying for assets.[268]

Further, infrastructure in all countries is subject to heavy government regulation. Investments are difficult to achieve without some sort of public support. Even privately owned assets are subject to various laws and monitoring by government agencies. Projects are complex and involve multiple parties. Because infrastructure services often become natural monopolies, detailed contracts are typically signed between public and private parties to ensure the reliable operation and delivery of services as well as guaranteed payments to the investor. This makes infrastructure subject to a certain degree of political risk. Changing regulatory environments, new infrastructure policies, and political corruption can all bring down the value of an infrastructure investment.[269]

Governments can also change the prices, or tariffs, that users pay for infrastructure services. For example, in 2015, the

---

268 Inderst and Stewart, *Institutional Investment*, 8-9.
269 Ibid.

Airports Economic Regulatory Authority of India decided to reduce the charges for using airlines to use the Delhi International Airport (DIAL) by 78 percent. For Fraport, a transport company that held a 10 percent stake in the same airport, that represented a change that would "erase DIAL's net worth."[270]

BARRIERS TO PRIVATE SECTOR INVESTMENT IN INFRASTRUCTURE

A 2016 report by the McKinsey Center for Business and Environment outlines five critical barriers to attracting greater private sector capital to infrastructure. They are as follows: lack of viable funding models, lack of transparent project pipelines, high development and transaction costs, inadequate risk-adjusted returns, and unfavorable and uncertain regulations and policies. I will briefly discuss each of these barriers and how they play out in developing countries. [271]

LACK OF VIABLE FUNDING MODELS

It will be useful to distinguish between two concepts commonly used interchangeably: financing and funding. Because infrastructure is so expensive to build, it requires loads of up-front investment. To raise this capital, project developers can reach out to banks or private investors to borrow money or sell the asset for equity or a combination of both. This is called financing. Funding, however, is the money used to pay for infrastructure over time, either through fees paid directly from users or from government revenue raised through taxes.

---

270 O'DEA, "Emerging Markets."
271 Bielenberg et al., *Financing Change*, 3.

One way or another, funding has to come from the populations who actually use infrastructure services (unless the project is paid for by donors). This is how investors in infrastructure make returns on their investments.[272]

Any successful infrastructure project requires both financing and funding. One cannot exist without the other. Investors would never finance projects without the promise of adequate funding, and there would be no projects to fund without upfront financing. Households in developing countries by definition have lower income than the rest of the world. In short, they don't have as much money to pay for their infrastructure services, whether directly through tolls and utility bills or indirectly through taxation. This is the core reason why infrastructure investments in poor countries are so difficult. At the end of the day, as much money as pension funds, insurance companies, and sovereign wealth funds have, the people of these countries are the ones who will have to pay them back.

Assets have to create revenue, but many people in low-income countries can't afford to pay prices high enough to even cover cost, let alone an additional charge to generate a return on investment. In some countries, there is the risk people won't pay at all. Seventy percent of water in sub-Saharan Africa does not bring in any revenue because it is unmetered or stolen.[273] The funding problem is compounded when factoring the extra costs associated with making infrastructure sustainable. Investors and developers need to be compensated

---

272 Kline, "Answering."
273 Ibid.

for sustainability, but positive externalities, like less pollution and climate resistance, are very difficult to monetize.

LACK OF TRANSPARENT PROJECT PIPELINES

According to Tomás Serebrisky of the Inter-American Development Bank, closing the infrastructure gap is not as simple as building more assets. You have to pick the right ones. Because infrastructure is built to last for long periods of time, it has to match a country's specific development trajectory. Assets must correspond with the needs and demands of a population in order to be successful. Imagine you are an urban planner for a new city. If you wish for the city to have high density like Hong Kong, then infrastructure should be planned to service many people living in close proximity. Alternatively, if you wish for the city to have low density like Los Angeles and Atlanta, then roads, water pipes, and transmission lines will have to travel across a much larger geographical area. The latter would be far more expensive and inefficient. This isn't to say all cities should be modeled after Hong Kong, only to illustrate how closely related infrastructure is to other aspects of development planning.

Unfortunately, most countries do a poor job of assessing long-term infrastructure needs and creating long-term infrastructure plans. Even where these plans do exist, investors are usually left in the dark. This is a problem even in developed countries. Just half of the G20 nations publish official infrastructure pipelines. The absence of project pipelines is one of the greatest supply-sided barriers to closing infrastructure gaps. When projects aren't adequately planned out, every other step along the infrastructure development process suffers for it.[274]

At a very basic level, investors need to have an idea of what projects are available in what countries before they can even think about allocating their capital. Beyond that, information on specific geographies and sectors is needed for investors to hire local staff and find partners for credit evaluation and due diligence. Potential projects also need to be "bankable," which at minimum means they can deliver adequate risk-adjusted returns to justify private investment. Effective planning becomes even more important if projects are to incorporate sustainability standards and climate-change adaptation schemes.[275]

Many low-income countries lack the resources and personnel to develop high-quality project pipelines. Others lack the political will or vision to establish infrastructure planning agencies. Even if fund managers are able to raise enough money to specifically target infrastructure, they'll end up charging management fees and paying deal teams while waiting for actual projects to materialize. [276]

HIGH DEVELOPMENT AND TRANSACTION COSTS

Many public institutions in low-income countries have very limited expertise when working with private investments in large infrastructure projects. Successful deal making

---

274 G20 Development Working Group, *Report on Infrastructure Agenda.*
275 Bhattacharya et al., *Sustainable Infrastructure*, 55–56.
276 Ibid.

typically requires a formalized transaction stage. This is where each of the potential stakeholders hash out details governing how the project is planned, financed, built, operated, and maintained. Investors need to know whether prices for service provision will be guaranteed and if they will be held liable for demand risk and cost overruns. A series of bidding between potential investors is sometimes used to match the project with the best investor and developer team that can deliver it at the lowest cost. A lack of transparency and a general unfamiliarity with transaction stages make them costly in both time and resources.

Few standards exist for procurement processes and the ones that do are fragmented and inconsistent. Transaction details on design, engineering, and financing are individualized for each project rather than standardized, making it incredibly difficult for investors with limited time to assess which projects are most suitable for their needs. As a result, similar infrastructure projects can end up with wildly different capital costs. Because so few private infrastructure deals have been made in these countries, there is also a shortage of data on historical performance that investors require to make their decisions.

INADEQUATE RISK-ADJUSTED RETURNS

Different investors differ in their expectations for return and their tolerance for risk. Private equity-type fund managers may be willing to take on the high risks associated with sustainable infrastructure in emerging markets, but not all projects are capable of delivering the corresponding high rates of return they expect. In emerging markets, early stages of project implementation often face longer and more costly delays that can bring down returns. Incorporating sustainability introduces even greater costs and risks associated with new technologies. Large asset owners like pension funds interested in directly investing are more likely to accept lower rates of return, but they also prefer long-term, safer investments. This explains their historical involvement in brownfield projects in developed markets.[277]

In general, the additional risks associated with investing in developing countries cause investors to demand additional risk premiums. Macroeconomic instability, financial health of governing bodies, and liquidity of the asset all factor into how much more investors need to be compensated for providing debt or equity financing to infrastructure projects. For example, operating onshore wind turbines is actually cheaper in developing countries than in developed ones, but the cost of investing is 40 percent higher because of debt and equity financing are more expensive.[278] The relatively higher cost of financing for low-income countries and the lack of risk-adjusted returns for investors are two sides of the same coin. Both make infrastructure investments prohibitively difficult.

UNFAVORABLE REGULATIONS AND POLICIES
Regulatory environments to enforce contracts made in infrastructure deals are weaker in developing countries, as are the institutions needed for project implementation and monitoring. Political corruption is more rampant and policy

---

277 Sharma, "Infrastructure: An Emerging Asset Class."
278 Bhattacharya et al., *Sustainable Infrastructure*, 56-60.

environments are less stable. Lawmakers may facilitate infrastructure procurement and award contracts to less than credit-worthy operators out of a desire to further their political careers. The threat of sudden, unilateral policy decision that affect investments is higher. Imagine purchasing a fossil-fuel-based power plant in a country that decides to go green and phase out carbon emissions right after.[279]

Each of these barriers contributes to a vicious cycle. Institutional and regulatory weakness leads to the absence of infrastructure planning and high-quality, actionable project pipelines. The lack of a pipeline raises financing costs and excludes private investors. Higher financing and capital costs lead to higher project costs. Higher project costs prevent infrastructure development, and the infrastructure gap keeps countries vulnerable and poor.

CRISIS RISK

Climate change, pandemics, and violent conflict pose their own risks. If assets can be physically destroyed by a flood or a militant group, that's really all an investor needs to know to steer clear of the entire region. In 2012, the World Bank had to suspend a rural electrification project in Mali because of civil unrest and conflict. The World Bank was also counting on the Malian Agency for the Development of Household Energy and Rural Electrification (AMADER) to help screen local contractor companies to build and implement the project. Because of the conflict, many members of AMADER left office, compromising the World Bank's ability to work with

---

279 Ibid.

local stakeholders. Can you see why an infrastructure project like this was financed by donors and a multilateral development bank rather than a private institutional investor? [280]

Why do these risks matter so much? At the end of the day, institutional investors are not interested in paying for positive externalities, nor should they be. Their sole concern lies in meeting their liabilities and honoring their obligations to their stakeholders. Pension funds have to ensure retirement checks for their members. Insurance companies have to pay out claims. Sovereign wealth funds have to steward riches for future generations. If infrastructure assets don't deliver adequate risk-adjusted returns, these institutions simply won't get involved.[281]

But if the infrastructure gap is not closed, countries will only become more vulnerable to global crises. Resources will become increasingly strained, greater populations will be displaced, industries will be disrupted, and tensions will follow. Unless action is taken now to find ways to mitigate them, the risks associated with developing water, energy, transportation, and telecommunications assets will only rise. Planning, implementation, and transaction costs will only go up. For many of the same reasons, the need for infrastructure services is also going to grow. The problem lies in finding ways align investor preferences with design specifications at each stage of the investment process and break the vicious cycle once and for all.

---

280 Runde, Moser, and Nealer, *Barriers*, 15-16.
281 Inderst and Stewart, *Institutional Investment*, 8.

9

RETHINKING THE ROLE OF GOVERNMENT

―――

Governments bear a lion's share of the responsibility when it comes to curating an amenable policy environment for private institutional investment in infrastructure. According to Georg Inderst, a well-known advisor to pension funds and international organizations, most developing countries simply do not have the kind of rigorous standards, rule of law, and regulatory strength necessary to facilitate this process. But with the right policy changes and the right help, it's entirely possible for governments to change that. To illustrate this point, we go back to Egypt, where radical shifts in government policy have altered the country's energy outlook forever.

CRIPPLED BY SUBSIDIES
In the years prior to the Arab Spring, Egypt had built up a long history of poor energy planning and ineffective policy. The government under President Mubarak created a plan

to generate new electricity capacity according to 10 percent annual growth in demand. Actual growth ended up exceeding 12 percent due to extremely high population growth, and the country fell wildly short of meeting its energy needs. The political instability that ensued nearly bankrupted public coffers, and the government became unable to honor its contracts with natural gas companies hired to supply the nation's power. At the same time, the new administration was unable to secure loans from international banks, cutting off its ability to construct new power plants.[282]

The greatest failure of the Egyptian government was its policymaking around subsidies. For over fifty years, fossil fuels were heavily subsidized, and prices were held at artificially low levels.[283] For context, the price of diesel bottomed out at around fourteen cents per liter, compared to ninety-five cents in neighboring countries.[284] More was spent by the Egyptian government budget on energy subsidies than on social protection, health, and education expenditures combined.[285] While subsidies are typically used by public authorities to support spending by the poor, in this situation (and many others), they were actually disproportionately benefitting the wealthy. After all, it was the rich who owned the most houses, used the most air conditioning, and drove the most vehicles.[286]

---

282 Ismail, "Power Generation."
283 Schwartztein, "Egypt's Crisis."
284 Ibid.
285 ESMAP, *Maximizing Finance*.
286 Ibid.

Subsidies encouraged heavy fuel consumption because of the artificially low energy prices. Subsequently, all competition in the industry was killed, and the existing power utilities were operating at a complete loss. Cost recovery in the energy sector was only 30 percent. It wasn't an industry that was viable enough to invest in because there was no money to be made. Even if investments were made into new infrastructure, the energy produced could not be sold at prices that would provide a return on investment because it wouldn't be competitive with low, subsidized prices. It was no wonder private investors wanted no part in Egypt's energy situation, no matter how desperately the population needed it. What's worse, the decades-long practice of wasteful subsidies had become a politically sensitive issue, and policymakers were afraid to make changes and risk losing their leadership positions.[287]

The situation described above created something called offtake risk, the single greatest impediment to private investment in energy infrastructure. Essentially, offtake risk is the risk that an investor-owned power producer won't get paid for its energy output. Utility companies, often state-owned, are usually the ones that purchase power from power producers and then sell it to customers. Because of this, they are called offtakers. If the power producer gets paid profitably, then it is a viable investment. If utility and distribution companies are in terrible financial health and can't make any money because of government subsidies, as was the case in Egypt, then energy infrastructure becomes a terrible investment.[288]

---

287 ESMAP, *Maximizing Finance*.
288 Center for Energy Finance, "Offtake Risk."

Because power is often seen as a public good, there are often significant shortfalls in cost recovery. If the government decides to subsidize energy purchases, the consumer does not pay the entire cost of the power they consume. This makes offtakers heavily reliant on the government for continuous funding which can be crippling for the energy industry as a whole. Subsidized energy can support populations up to a certain point, but the sector inevitably becomes unviable in the long term. When it comes to unleashing more investment in energy infrastructure in the poorest parts of the world, the single most important task is to enhance the viability of the offtaker by ensuring cost recovery.[289]

By 2013, with the country unable to produce its own electricity and lacking the cash to import additional fuel resources, Egypt was hurtling toward a terrible energy crisis. Service providers started scheduling regular blackouts in order to ration fuel supply. The toll enacted on commercial and civilian life was substantial. Small businesses saw significant downturns in production and citizens saw major disruptions to everyday life.[290]

A MIRACLE IN THE DESERT

It wasn't until the summer of 2014 that Egypt's energy crisis showed the first signs of turning around. By then, the country was desperate for change. But before any investments could be made into new energy assets, the policy environment needed to be seriously reworked. That meant putting

---

289 Bhattacharya et al., *Sustainable Infrastructure*.
290 Kingsley, "Egypt Suffers."

subsidy reform on the table. Fortunately, the government had help. The World Bank's Energy Sector Management Assistance Program (ESMAP) intervened to provide technical assistance and advise the authorities on how to proceed with reforms.[291]

ESMAP provided simulations of different reform scenarios and their potential consequences. Through this process, policymakers became convinced subsidies could be phased out without causing runaway inflation or recession. It was well known that changes to energy prices would have impacts on Egypt's citizens. The purchase of fuel made up 12 percent of household expenditure for poor Egyptians. Naturally, they would be the hardest hit once subsidies were removed. But the government was able to come up with a social protection plan to help its population adjust. The money saved from not having to pay out subsidies would be redirected toward direct income support for the poor and spending on health and education. With these preparations in place, the country was ready for the ambitious and forward-thinking reforms it implemented in July of 2014.[292]

By 2015, public healthcare and education expenditures exceeded energy subsidies for the first time. Again, with the help of the World Bank, Egypt set up the $400 million Strengthening Social Safety Net Project. This led to two direct cash transfer programs called Takaful and Karama that supported nine million poor Egyptians through the

---

291 ESMAP, *Maximizing Finance*.
292 Ibid.

transition. By the year 2018, spending on social safety nets for the bottom fifth of income earners had doubled.[293]

"Through the Takaful pension, I was able to begin my small baking business at home. I bought two sacks of flour and started baking bread. People come and buy bread from me, so I don't need to leave my house," said Sabah, a woman from Qena, Upper Egypt. Because assistance was mostly targeted at women, the programs had the added effects of increasing intra-household decision making and improving food and health outcomes. All this because the government didn't have to spend such exorbitant sums on subsidizing energy.[294]

The reform scenarios laid the groundwork for a transformation of the energy sector, but there was still work needed to be done. To ensure the long-term stability of Egypt's energy situation, The World Bank provided a three-part series of developmental policy loans worth a total of $3.15 billion. Development policy loans provide countries with money specifically targeted at helping them adopt better policies for growth and development. It isn't money directly spent on fighting poverty, improving health outcomes, or building infrastructure. Rather, it is money meant to change the way countries govern themselves and support policy environments more amenable to achieving those outcomes.[295]

The first loan helped Egyptian policymakers develop strategies to manage the loads of debt it had accumulated under

---

293 Ibid.
294 World Bank, "Cash Transfers."
295 ESMAP, *Maximizing Finance*.

heavy subsidies. It also helped set up an independent regulator that would oversee electricity law. The second loan helped raise electricity tariffs by 33 percent and started the development of policies to promote private investment in renewable energy power generation. The third and final loan had electricity tariffs up by 40 percent and increased the transparency of Egypt's main electric utility. The country also launched its first feed-in tariff scheme for solar and wind projects. Feed-in tariffs are policy mechanisms that offer long-term contracts to renewable energy producers with the price certainty necessary to ensure the viability of long-term energy infrastructure investments for the private sector.[296]

This new policy environment was far more amenable to attracting private sector capital. New renewable energy laws and regulations allowed for a more competitive bidding process for power producers. Most importantly, the energy sector was now commercially viable. Utility companies were forced to reduce their losses and become more cost efficient. At the same time, fossil fuel prices began to rise, causing the renewables sector to become competitive and a much more credible investment. There was no more cheap fuel to steal away demand from sustainably produced solar and wind power. The country was ready to open itself up to the floods of private capital seeking strong and reliable infrastructure investments.[297]

The government, with the help of the World Bank's International Finance Corporation, assembled nine international

---

296 Ibid.
297 Ibid.

banks to invest in Egypt's renewables, a groundbreaking development. This eventually led to the building of the Benban Solar Park, a $653 million project. The new infrastructure created over 6,000 local jobs and now provides roughly 1,560 MW of eco-friendly and cost-effective power to over 350,000 homes. As a side-effect, the project also eliminated two million tons of green-house-gas emissions. That's equivalent to removing 400,000 cars from the road.[298]

To allay any additional fears investors in the solar park had regarding uncertainty in the policy environment, the World Bank's Multilateral Investment Guarantee Agency worked directly with investors to provide $210 million in political risk insurance. That means, in the event that changes in Egypt's laws or regulations interfere with returns on infrastructure assets, investors would be covered against losses. This program made renewables an even more viable investment.[299]

THE POSSIBILITY OF CHANGE
It is worthwhile to take a moment to consider the full magnitude of Egypt's experience with energy. Private investors won't touch infrastructure in developing countries because the risks are too great. One of the biggest policy impediments keeping those risks in place is the high cost of energy subsidies, a pervasive problem that isn't unique to Egypt. The IMF estimated total costs of energy subsidies were as high as

---

298 Ibid.
299 Ibid.

$5.3 trillion in 2015, 97 percent of which was directed toward fossil fuels.[300]

Like in Egypt, the benefits of global fuel subsidies largely accrue to higher income groups, the very ones who seek to keep them in place. Getting rid of these subsidies could lower global greenhouse emissions by *20 percent*. Countries would save trillions of dollars in fiscal expenditures that could be redirected to less regressive social protections and sustainable infrastructure. It would be a major step toward minimizing the continuing effects of the climate crisis and building an enabling environment for a green energy revolution.[301]

Egypt's story proves *risk can be removed*. But doing so requires expanding the scope of reform beyond infrastructure itself to underlying policies and governance structures. Notice how the participation of the World Bank didn't concern directly financing renewable energy projects. We've already established how the MDBs simply do not have the resources to close the infrastructure gap on their own. What they do have is experience, technical expertise, and enough money to lend to countries that want to change their policy environments and become more viable for private sector investment. By providing money in the millions and billions for development policy loans and political risk insurance, the World Bank helped Egypt open itself up to potential trillions.

By getting rid of its subsidies and redirecting funds, Egypt was able to focus its spending on the poorest populations. It

---

300 Coady et al., "Global Energy Subsidies," 5.
301 Bhattacharya et al., *Sustainable Infrastructure*, 64.

stopped wasting resources on keeping energy cheap for the wealthy and started providing direct income support to those who actually needed it. This made it easier for everyone in the country to afford energy at competitive prices and made the entire energy sector commercially viable. The investors in the Benban Solar Park weren't necessarily concerned with the environment or with boosting economic growth, but the project was able to generate local jobs, reduce carbon emissions, and provide millions of people with electricity to improve their quality of life.[302]

Egypt still gets the vast majority of its energy from oil and natural gas. But now, with all the right policies in place and the price of renewables dropping considerably, the nation is primed for a green revolution. The government's aim is to get 42 percent of its electricity supply from renewable sources by 2025, a goal that would truly have been laughable in 2013. With the right help, even more countries like Egypt can become safe enough for institutional investors to move even more of their capital into infrastructure.[303]

At the same time, investors must be proactive in working together with governments and the development banks to replicate the Egyptian experience. According to Jim Yong Kim, the twelfth president of the World Bank, most investors in infrastructure don't even know products like political risk insurance and development policy even exist. He tells a story of an annual infrastructure investment meeting he attended. In front of a crowd of four hundred of the

---

302 Egypt Today, "Benban Solar Project."
303 Scheier, "World's Largest."

world's most prominent investors, he asked how many of them thought policy environments had a direct effect on their evaluation of infrastructure projects in emerging economies. Every hand was raised. He then asked how many of them knew what a development policy loan was. Only about five hands remained up.[304]

Yes, investing in developing countries is risky, but investors and policymakers must be willing to take a closer look at who they can partner with and how they can work together to make it happen. If the failure of emerging markets infrastructure assets is simply treated as a forgone conclusion, the world will never be able to channel enough capital into places that need it most. The clock is ticking on climate change, and we need to look for solutions like the ones that worked for Egypt. It's possible. As difficult as it may seem, it's possible, and investors have to know it's possible before they begin to act.

---

[304] *Milken Institute*, "Filling."

10

PUBLIC-PRIVATE PARTNERSHIPS

The story of energy in Egypt showcases how underlying policy environments like fuel subsidies can form serious bottlenecks to attracting greater investment in infrastructure. But even if countries hobbled by subsidies were to remove them, there is still no guarantee they will have the institutional capacity necessary to *make infrastructure deals*. Successfully executing a transaction with private investors for new infrastructure is incredibly difficult, nearly impossible for countries without previous experience to do on their own. It isn't as simple as getting everybody in a room together, signing a few agreements, and popping a bottle of champagne to seal the deal (although even this would probably be very difficult to achieve). Each of the many stakeholders in an infrastructure deal has to be confident their needs and goals will be met. A laundry list of considerations has to be made, including but not limited to pricing, capital costs, financing arrangements, guarantees, regulations, and environmental and social effects. Resolving each of these is notoriously difficult.[305]

Public-private partnership (PPP), a catch-all term for projects where public authorities and private companies collaborate to split up the risks and responsibilities for the financing, building, and operation of infrastructure. Without transparent regulatory environments and robust investment frameworks, private investors will be incredibly wary of entering into transactions in developing markets. It is up to the public sector to establish these enabling conditions and generate real incentives for private investment and international support. The problem is many countries either aren't capable of executing these partnerships or aren't willing to put in the time and resources necessary to learn how. For this reason, PPPs in developing countries are incredibly hard to coordinate.[306]

Fortunately, in the same way Egypt was able to accomplish policy reform, developing countries can now put forward quality investment frameworks with the support of the right programs and partners. Given how complex and difficult infrastructure projects are, closing the gap will be impossible without close collaboration between several different players. For example, institutional investors may provide the primary source of financing while donor funds provide guarantees and blended finance to lower overall investment risk. Multilateral development banks and international policy organizations can provide technical and policy expertise

---

305 Bhattacharya et al., *Sustainable Infrastructure*.
306 Ibid.

to facilitate deal execution. Governments, meanwhile, should maintain a legal and regulatory environment that will protect all stakeholders.[307]

Creating the enabling conditions for each partner to fulfill its unique role is the single most important task to advance the global agenda on sustainable infrastructure. The following sections will detail case studies of successful solar power PPPs in Zambia and South Africa that demonstrate the necessary steps to complete stable, predictable, and efficient infrastructure investment deals.

SCALING SOLAR

In October of 2019, Japanese energy giant Univergy announced it would invest $200 million in solar power in Zambia. The new projects would add 200 megawatts of electricity capacity to the national grid. Barely half a decade ago, when the South African nation was going through its worst power crisis ever, such a headline would've been completely unthinkable. And yet this investment from Japan's private sector isn't an isolated instance. Despite the odds, a revolution in solar power has been happening in Zambia, and the country's energy sector has opened itself up to the world.[308]

Zambia has historically done slightly better than its neighboring countries when it comes to energy access, but levels are still incredibly low. Just 31 percent of the population is

---

307 Ibid.
308 Ranjan, "Japan's Univergy."

connected to the electricity grid.[309] In rural areas, access is virtually nonexistent at just 4 percent.[310] Climate change has had a particularly devastating effect on energy woes. Over the past decade, Zambia has been caught in one of the most debilitating droughts of the century.[311]

The vast majority of the Zambia's electricity generation comes from hydroelectric sources. The Kariba Dam, the world's largest man-made reservoir, supplies about half of the country's power on its own.[312] Because of climate change, rainfall in Zambia has declined significantly and water levels in Lake Kariba are at all-time lows.[313] Hydropower production at the Kariba Dam is now at just a quarter of its capacity.[314] Zesco, the national utility, began implementing a power rationing scheme called load-shedding to manage the declining supply. These deliberate power outages were as long as sixteen hours a day in 2019.[315]

Without electricity, water utilities have struggled to pump water from the Kafue River to residential areas, and municipal water supply has dwindled. Customers received notices from Lusaka Water and Sewerage company that read, "Kindly be advised that every time our pump stations are

---

309 Solar Aid, "Zambia Drought."
310 Ibid.
311 Johnson, "Zambia Warns."
312 Gibbons, "Zambians Brace."
313 Ibid.
314 Ibid.
315 Haria and Ahmed, "Increasing Tariffs."

loadshedded, you will be experiencing erratic water supply. Make it a habit to store emergency water."[316]

Zambia has had an incredibly difficult time expanding its generation capacity and diversifying its sources of electricity beyond hydropower, making it particularly vulnerable to climate impacts like droughts. In 2016, with the country in shambles due to the protracted energy crisis, Zambian President Edgar Lungu implored his leaders to explore new ways to meet energy needs. What resulted was one of the most remarkable instances of multilateral collaboration on delivering sustainable energy infrastructure in modern history.[317]

In collaboration with the International Finance Corporation (IFC), the country was enrolled in an experimental program called Scaling Solar. It was an attempt to attract private sector capital to build Zambia's first large-scale solar plants. And it worked. A total of forty-eight of the world's foremost renewable energy development companies submitted bids to build two massive solar projects that would bring an additional 600 MW to the country. It was a completely unprecedented result.[318]

One of the foremost barriers to private sector involvement in emerging markets infrastructure is the lack of a competitive process. If a single developer offers to build a solar power plant, the cost of financing is inevitably higher than if multiple developers compete with each other to win the project.

---

316 Phiri, "Load-shedding."
317 Rio, *Auctions*.
318 Ibid.

A lack of transparency and organization also drives up the cost of financing. Without any clear understanding of what each part of the project will look like and what kinds of risks they'll be exposed to, investors are completely unwilling to supply financing.[319]

Prior to Scaling Solar, renewable energy developers in Zambia were being offered interest rates upwards of 30 percent, which is completely commercially unviable. Because the developers make money by selling the generated electricity to Zambia's national utility, the higher costs of financing would translate to higher prices of energy for consumers. When solar power is prohibitively expensive, it's of little use to the population. Finally, because of a general lack of expertise within the country, executing a single transaction would take an incredibly long time, sometimes upwards of five years.[320]

Scaling Solar brought a formalized, competitive auction process to the table. With the help of technical expertise from the International Finance Corporation, simple and standardized tender documents were created so competitive bids could be easily compared with each other. This drastically decreased the time spent negotiating a final deal. The World Bank also brought with it a suite of financing products to help reduce the risk exposure to investors. For example, because it offered to take first losses on construction and project development, private investors felt much more comfortable submitting bids.[321]

---

319 Ibid.
320 Ibid.
321 IFC, *Scaling Solar*.

The program did an incredible job of setting up the solar energy projects. By the time private investors were involved, the sites for the power plants had been identified, feasibility studies were completed, and legal and tax diligence was done. It was an investment ripe for the picking. Without all that preparation, investors would have no way of deciding whether or not they could secure a return. Instead, they had all the numbers they needed to plug into their models and move forward with a bid.[322]

The entire process took only two years. By 2019, electrons were flowing from the two fully developed, fully operational solar projects. Prior to Scaling Solar, solar energy in Zambia was sold at prices around twenty-four cents per kilowatt hour. The two winning bids for these two projects were for 6.02 cents per kilowatt hour and 7.84 cents per kilowatt hour. Those prices were not only the lowest Africa had ever seen, but they also were the lowest ever recorded anywhere in the world. Over the course of twenty-five years, it estimated Zambia will save $163 million on energy for each plant. That's serious development progress.[323]

But perhaps what is even more miraculous than this initial success is the country's newfound ability to implement the program at scale. With two projects under its belt, the country is already in preparations for the second round of Scaling Solar. Zambia's population is slated to benefit massively from the

program is something that has the potential to be replicated across the entire continent of Africa.[324]

Philippe Le Houéru, chief executive officer at the IFC, said, "It is now possible for governments across sub-Saharan Africa to look first to solar power as a solution for inexpensive, quick-to-build power—something unimaginable outside of South Africa until now."[325]

RENEWABLE ENERGY INDEPENDENT POWER PRODUCERS PROGRAM (REIPPP)

One of the greatest achievements of the South African energy industry in recent memory is the Renewable Energy Independent Power Producers Program (REIPPP). Like Scaling Solar, the program was designed as a vehicle for securing electricity capacity from Independent Power Producers (IPP) by introducing a bidding process for contracts.[326]

Here's how it worked. In August of 2011, an initial Request for Proposals (RFP) was sent out to domestic and international investors. Fifty-three bids were submitted, of which twenty-eight were selected to build 1,415 megawatts of power generating capacity. Second and third rounds of bidding commenced shortly after. By 2014, a total of sixty-four projects were awarded to the private sector. Fourteen billion dollars of investment was committed, creating the potential to generate 3922 megawatts of renewable power. That year, IPPs generated

---

324 IFC, *Scaling Solar*.
325 IFC, "Scaling Solar Delivers."
326 Eberhard, Kolker, and Leigland, *South Africa's Renewable*.

enough capacity to power the equivalent of 700,000 homes and avoided the release of 2.3 million tons of carbon dioxide. At the same time, the bidding process pushed down prices for solar and wind energy. Over one hundred shareholder entities participated in the IPP program, representing a wide range of international and domestic banks, insurers, and development finance institutions.[327]

REIPPPP was immensely successful. In just three years, South Africa secured more investment for independent power generation than the entire continent of Africa in the past twenty years. Kannan Lakmeeharan represented Eskom, the South African electric public utility, in several power purchase agreements under this program.

"I think it was a great example of having a very transparent public procurement process, very clear objectives, and engaging well with the stakeholders," he told me.

Several key lessons for emerging markets can be learned from the REIPPPP on program management and program design. First, autonomous, well-governed institutions need to be set up so they can interface transparently and directly with private sector investors. The IPP Office was established under the leadership of the Department of Energy and the Development Bank of South Africa with the intent of being a largely ad hoc institution. That arrangement brought extensive expertise with public-private partnerships and credibility with both public and private investors. The IPP Office was trusted enough to secure enough resources to

---

327 Ibid.

appoint experienced advisors who brought international best practices to the table. It also allowed a greater focus on problem-solving rather than solving bureaucratic issues, while still maintaining the quality and transparency of a government agency.[328]

In an article written for his current employer, McKinsey, Kannan and his fellow authors outline five key functions that can be carried out by such autonomous institutions.

1. Identifying the deals that could benefit from private-capital financing, as part of a national or sectoral portfolio of projects.
2. Building and publishing the deal pipeline to create transparency and certainty on upcoming transactions.
3. Building a robust, early perspective on the viability of all projects in the pipeline to focus resources on viable deals.
4. Providing project-development funding to selected projects, allowing expertise to be hired to structure projects in a commercially viable manner.
5. Designing and implementing a sequential stage-gated approach to manage implementation of each project—so allowing for course correction as well as relevant stakeholder alignment and action at each stage gate.[329]

Each of these functions played a critical role in the success of REIPPP. Governments and development finance institutions in emerging markets across the globe ought to consider how they might set up their own institutions to facilitate private

---

328 Ibid.
329 Hussain et al., "Unlocking."

sector investment in infrastructure. Bringing the right kind of governance and experienced advisors to the table will be critical to organizing successful projects and delivering on sustainability objectives.

Second, private sponsors and financiers are eager to invest in renewable energy projects as long as procurement frameworks are well designed. In the case of REIPPP, several features contributed to swiftness and willingness with which contracts were awarded. The program had a rolling bid-window format whereby lessons learned from each bid process could be applied before the beginning of the next. Each of the initial three bid-windows for REIPPP increased competitive pressure, reduced prices, and built confidence for the subsequent round. Average solar photovoltaic tariffs decreased 68 percent and wind tariffs decreased 42 percent over the three rounds of bidding. The structure of the bidding process also allowed for multiple winners at the same time, serving as an extra incentive for private investors to participate.[330]

Third, REIPPP required bids to be underwritten with both debt and equity, which removed the ability of competitive tenders to under-bid. Because borrowing money (debt) is typically much cheaper than committing cash capital upfront (equity), bidders can use all debt to win contracts. This undercuts the competitive process and damages the market. REIPPP was also created in alignment with the South African National Development Plan, a recognition of the relationship between the country's most important development goals and the contributions made by IPPs in areas

---

330 Eberhard, Kolker, and Leigland, *South Africa's Renewable*, 2.

like energy access, education, job creation, and the economic participation of disadvantaged communities.[331]

Finally, the REIPPP showed that it can be feasible to require investors to put money toward socioeconomic development and social progress. The primary motivation of private investors in any infrastructure transaction obviously is to turn a profit. In some cases, a portion of their funds can be allocated to certain non-financial goals like local community development or sustainability, but the budget for this kind of spending is usually discretionary and very small. To be clear, I am speaking of goals that are explicitly social or developmental in nature, not of the various development outcomes that result from the provision of infrastructure services. The achievement of these goals, in any at all, typically depends on the goodwill of the investor.

This was not the case with REIPPP. Public infrastructure agencies evaluate bids for contracts through multiple factors, but the primary criterion is the price, or tariff, at which the investor/developer team can operate the asset. In the case of energy, it would be the price the power producer accepts from a utility company for the purchase of its electricity generation. In the case of REIPPP, however, bids were evaluated not only on price, but also on compliance with specific "economic development requirements."

In order to win contracts under the program, bidders had to demonstrate how their investments would promote "job growth, domestic industrialization, community development,

---

331 Ibid.

and black economic empowerment." For example, all projects had to have at least 40 percent participation from South African entities in order to be bid compliant. For international investors, that meant structuring the project in ways that would promote rather than take employment and economic prosperity from the region. Bidders also had to submit a plan that identified the needs of local communities surrounding the asset and offered a strategy for working with donor and grant funding to meet those needs.[332] In total, economic and social development factors accounted for 30 percent of bid value.

Ashwin West is an Investment Director at African Infrastructure Investment Managers (AIIM), a private equity fund that participated in REIPPP. In our recent conversation, he told me about how his firm responded to these economic development requirements.

"With the REIPPP, there was commitment that the portfolio companies had to contribute a percentage of their revenue toward socioeconomic development," he said. "That's an obligation of the program, and, of course, we absolutely have to meet those obligations, and we put a lot of effort into how we do it."

According to Ashwin, AIIM is by no means an impact investor, but that doesn't mean it doesn't pay close attention to development outcomes. That becomes especially true with programs like REIPPP that make social spending non-discretionary.

---

332 Ibid.

"Our primary objective is to deliver a market return for our investors, but we obviously see the benefit of having some sort of impact. What we will always do is try to have some positive social impact in the communities we're investing in, and we'll try to build that into the business case."

Other programs in private investment infrastructures should model the REIPPP and evaluate bids on both their socioeconomic and financial merits. However, to achieve maximum impact and efficiency, non-price criteria and social standards need to be well-defined and consistent. Robust mechanisms for monitoring and enforcing performance also have to be set up. One of the shortcomings of REIPPP was the confusion that development requirements caused investors. Little guidance was provided on how to prepare the plan for local economic development and how it was going to be evaluated. These issues related to inconsistency and vagueness make submitting proposals more difficult for investors and may eventually result in correspondingly inconsistent development outcomes. Part of the role of multilateral development banks and autonomous infrastructure agencies can be to define these standards in clear, measurable terms.[333]

DEVELOPING INFRASTRUCTURE AS AN ASSET CLASS

Both Scaling Solar and REIPPP were designed to facilitate direct, project-level equity and debt. "Direct" means investors are putting money into the infrastructure project without the assistance of an outside fund manager. Asset owners (pension funds, sovereign wealth funds, etc.) can either work directly

---

333 Ibid.

with project developers to invest or they can hire third-party asset managers (private equity funds, hedge funds, etc.) to make deals for them. "Project-level" means investors are investing into the asset itself rather than through debt or equity securities of a corporation. It's the difference between owning a portion of a solar power plant and owning the stock of a utility company. Under this structure, investors provide capital based on the risk-profile of the specific asset and earn returns supported by that asset's cash flows rather than a corporate balance sheet.[334]

Though this financing structure is the most common way for private institutions to invest in infrastructure, private financing can actually come in a variety of forms. Depending on the preference of any individual investor, different kinds of financing instruments (debt or equity), investment vehicles (publicly listed and private/unlisted), and investment routes (stocks, corporate bonds, project bonds, direct loans, etc.) may be more or less appealing. For example, OECD research found that asset owners tend to prioritize long-term capital appreciation and are thus more likely to invest in illiquid, project-level assets. Asset managers, in contrast, tend to like liquidity, so they to invest more in securitized products like infrastructure stocks and infrastructure bonds that can be easily bought and sold.[335]

Unfortunately, many of these different investment instruments, vehicles, and routes are not well developed. Most deals are confined to unlisted, project-level debt and equity.

---
334 US PREF, *Renewable Energy Finance Fundamentals*.
335 OECD, *Green Infrastructure*.

The unavailability of other methods of investing is a massive inhibitor to attracting larger pools of private capital to infrastructure. Certain institutions may only have the capacity to invest through one specific method, whether because regulations restrict other methods or because of a lack of expertise and capacity. The more challenging it is to invest via preferred methods, the less likely institutional investors will be to get involved at all. These underdevelopments in these capital market structures have prevented infrastructure from becoming a fully-fledged asset class of its own.[336]

Securitization, in particular, is a method of packaging infrastructure assets into standardized, liquid products that is seriously underutilized. Essentially, securitization allows an asset's cash flows to be portioned off into individual investments that can be distributed among investors with different risk and return preferences. It can help diversify and pool risks so that private financiers can come together and invest in projects they otherwise wouldn't invest in on their own. As the market for these securities grows, increased trading can lower the liquidity risk of infrastructure investments, making them much more attractive to investors who may want to exit on short notice.[337]

THE INFORMATION GAP

Infrastructure's struggle to become an asset class is related to another serious problem known as the "information gap." Simply put, the more information that investors have access

---

336 Bhattacharya et al., *Sustainable Infrastructure*, 93-95.
337 Ibid.

to, the easier it will be for them to invest. Clear and consistent data can provide a much better picture of what risk-return profiles will be like. Toll-road owners want to know how many vehicles travel in a certain area over different periods of time and what kinds of rules and regulations govern traffic. Energy investors want to know how well other power generating assets have performed. This kind of data can help credit-risk agencies assess the risks associated with any particular asset, which in turn can help dealmakers set prices and interest rates. Unfortunately, this kind of data isn't well collected and published in many countries, especially developing ones.[338]

Information related to previous investments is also sparse and inconsistent. Part of the reason why investments in other asset classes like government bonds or corporate stocks is so much more sophisticated is because the massive volume of historical data that is available. Without historical infrastructure projects to compare new investment opportunities to, investors will struggle to structure deals in ways they know will be successful. The standardization of project templates, as was the case for both Scaling Solar and REIPPP, can improve the flow of information to investors and help them evaluate projects using consistent criteria.[339]

The creation of benchmarks based on the historical returns of infrastructure investments can also help in this regard. Equity fund managers can compare the performance of their funds to benchmarks like the S&P 500 index. The same exists

---
338 OECD, *Breaking Silos*.
339 Ibid.

for a variety of bond funds. These indices help inform the decisions of asset owners and asset managers during the asset allocation process. In the same way, a benchmark for infrastructure performance would provide institutional investors with a success metric and a way to evaluate their long-term objectives with historical returns.[340]

The information gap should be addressed through global initiatives to share knowledge and data on project preparation and project performance with investors across the globe. MDBs and international organizations like the UN and the OECD can play a particularly important role when it comes to these initiatives. The Global Infrastructure Hub, established by the G20, is one such platform that seeks to connect governments and institutional investors through the widespread dissemination of data on both public and private infrastructure projects. It helps to match investors with projects they may not have otherwise been aware of. As more information becomes available, the market for infrastructure investments will become much more standardized and competitive. Once pricing and risks become more transparent, private sector investors will find it much easier to participate.[341]

ASSET RECYCLING

As we've already established, institutional investors tend to prefer low-risk, brownfield assets that already have steady income streams. Because of the higher risks associated with

---

340 Bhattacharya et al., *Sustainable Infrastructure*, 93–95.
341 Ibid.

construction and project preparation, institutional investors may shy away from getting involved in the earlier stages of infrastructure development. At the same time, the greatest need for infrastructure is in new assets. This is known as the greenfield problem, something that seriously inhibits the potential of private finance to help close the global infrastructure gap.[342]

Rectifying the disparity between institutional investor preferences and the need for new assets could put an end to chronic underinvestment in infrastructure. A few countries have experimented with a process called asset recycling that could be a potential solution to the greenfield problem. Here's how it works. Governments, commercial banks and MDBs take on the additional risk associated with earlier stages of the project, before the asset begins generating yields. Once the asset becomes operational and has a steady income stream, it can be sold off or leased to institutional investors through a public-private partnership. This then frees up budget space to develop even more new infrastructure. The private investors then take responsibility for upgrading and improving the infrastructure while collecting its cash flows. The potential for bond financing at this stage is huge. If the infrastructure is mature and credit-worthy, bonds can be issued to a much wider range of investors than during initial phases.[343]

If governments and development banks were to keep all the infrastructure on their new balance sheets, they would soon

---

342 Ibid.
343 KPMG, *Global Infrastructure*, 1.

run out of fiscal space to take on new projects. Institutional investors have much more available capital to hold these assets for long periods of time. By passing off roads, bridges, and power plants to pension funds and insurance companies, the public sector can continue developing infrastructure without fear of running into budget problems. Investors can confidently invest in infrastructure without taking on excessive risks.[344]

This method of delivering infrastructure is most prominently featured in Australia's Asset Recycling Initiative (ARI). The ARI was a federal program designed to incentivize Australian states to monetize their assets and use the proceeds for the development of new infrastructure. A number of major public infrastructure assets were sold or leased under this system, including several electric utilities in New South Wales and the Port of Melbourne in Victoria. The majority of investors that participated in the ARI were Australian pension funds and asset managers, though several international funds formed consortiums to co-sponsor projects.[345]

I recently spoke with Rajiv Sharma, research director at the Stanford Global Projects Center and an expert on private investment in infrastructure about the merits of asset recycling.

"Ten years ago, pension funds wouldn't look at greenfield because of all of the extra risks associated with it," he told me. "My perspective on solving the greenfield infrastructure

---

344 Ibid.
345 Marsh & McLennan Companies, *Infrastructure Asset Recycling*.

issue in developing countries is to take a leaf out of some of the examples in Australia."

According to Rajiv, asset recycling could be a particularly attractive option for governments trying to stimulate their economies coming out of the COVID-19 crisis. The difficulty in developing regions lies in the lack of capacity to execute these transactions.

"The challenge is having a government entity that has the sophistication to be able to facilitate the transaction. The first step is to offer the brownfield assets in a way that generates the most capital for the government and then having the expertise to use that capital for a new project. The greenfield development can be structured in multiple ways. You could use a PPP to do it, or you could use just a general EPC contractor to do it. That's where having the expertise at the government level to understand the dynamics of the procurement is required."

Asset recycling may be a promising strategy for greenfield development, but it won't be a silver bullet. For one, the method depends on a government already owning a sizable quantity of assets that could potentially be sold. While this may be the case in most of the developed world and in emerging economies like China, India, Mexico, and Brazil, governments in less-developed countries are less likely to have such robust balance sheets. Without assets to monetize, these countries will struggle to generate enough capital for new infrastructure. Still, asset recycling is a relatively new concept, and its effectiveness may improve as governments and institutional investors become more sophisticated in their deal making.[346]

LEARNING AS MUCH AS WE CAN

Securitization assistance, knowledge-sharing platforms, and asset-recycling templates are precisely the kind of initiatives that aid can fund to catalyze private investment in infrastructure. These are the kinds of tools that make the process easier, something that must be done if we are to turn billions worth of funding into trillions worth of investments.[347]

As a whole, the world needs to *learn more* about infrastructure. How to invest in it, how to operate and manage it, how to regulate it, and how to ensure its social and environmental sustainability. Part of this is collecting and publishing more data, but, more importantly, it's about a global commitment to share knowledge and collaborate with one another. Countries that have found innovative ways to deliver infrastructure ought to spread their expertise to countries that are comparatively less experienced. Investors who have built up sophisticated infrastructure portfolios have to advise governments and other investors on how to make high-quality deals.

Simply put, we need to put aside our differences and work together. The global infrastructure gap won't be closed if every nation is left to their own devices. We need international solutions to international problems like pandemics and climate change. If countries can support one another

---

346 Ibid.
347 Inderst, "Financing Development."

through each of their individual infrastructure journeys, real and impactful change could be closer than ever.

11

THE OPPORTUNITY OF A LIFETIME

I believe that the pandemic has presented such an existential crisis – such a stark reminder of our fragility – that it has driven us to confront the global threat of climate change more forcefully and to consider how, like the pandemic, it will alter our lives.

—LARRY FINK

I remember the exact moment when the full reality of COVID-19 first hit me. It was the first week of March. I had just returned to school the night before, after spending the week of spring break back home in Palatine. Looking back, it was the last time for a while that life would feel "normal." My friends and I were sitting in a booth in the main dining hall at my university, talking about what everyone did over break. Occasionally, coronavirus would come up in conversation. At that time, the number of cases in all of the US were still in the hundreds, so we felt isolated enough not to feel worried.

Then we heard screams. "Check your email!" Everyone around me pulled out their phones, reading and rereading a message just sent to us by our chancellor. The university had cancelled in-person classes for the rest of the semester, and we were all expected to vacate the campus within five days. Barely half an hour after the email was sent out, I saw students walking around with suitcases, all packed and ready to go home. It felt surreal. An announcement like that today wouldn't have fazed anybody. But at that time, without any sort of understanding of what was about to happen to the country, it was almost unbelievable.

The year 2020 will go down in history as the year of the pandemic. In January, when news of COVID-19 spreading first came out, the rest of the world could never have imagined what was coming (although it might have if it listened to warnings from experts). Over the course of the year, millions of lives would be claimed by the virus and many millions more would contract it. Hospitals were overwhelmed. Businesses and schools were shut down. Travel ceased overnight. There may not be a single person on earth who wasn't in some way affected by the coronavirus. It was one of those years where the stories of each family's experiences will be passed on from generation to generation.[348]

Even as you are reading this right now, I'm sure you are remembering the exact moment you knew the pandemic was real—where you were, what you were doing, who you were with. Across the world, people of all backgrounds will remember. All of those details will forever be connected to

---

348 Law, "2 Million."

the year of the coronavirus. But beyond the quarantines, social distancing, and mask wearing (and the politics behind it all), a remarkable opportunity has emerged—an opportunity not only to rescue entire countries from the depths of economic depression, but to transition the world toward a more prosperous, sustainable future. It could change the way we remember 2020 forever.

A NEW, NEW DEAL

On October 29, 1929, a day memorialized in history as Black Tuesday, the American stock market crashed. The effects were tremendous. Economic woes flooded the United States and quickly spread to the rest of the world. Global GDP fell by an estimated 15 percent from 1929 to 1932.[349] It was like nothing the world had ever experienced before. At the height of the Great Depression, US unemployment rose to 25 percent, the highest ever recorded.[350] Destitute families were forced onto the streets by the masses. Riots erupted due to widespread frustration and a pervasive loss of hope. As Nick Taylor wrote in his book *American-Made: The Enduring Legacy of the WPA*, it was "the greatest crisis in history short of war."[351]

On July 2, 1932, as he accepted his nomination to the US presidency at the Democratic National Convention, Franklin Delano Roosevelt told the country, "I pledge you, I pledge myself, a new deal for the American people."[352] His pledge would manifest into a series of programs targeted at relief,

---
349 Lowenstein, "Economic History Repeating."
350 University of Washington, "The Great Depression."
351 Taylor, *American Made*.
352 Roosevelt, "Acceptance Speech."

reform, and recovery that would ultimately save the nation. The Public Works Administration was established, putting millions of unemployed Americans back to work. The PWA spent $3.3 billion to build over large public infrastructure projects, an amount that was over 165 percent of the federal government's revenues in 1933.[353] Over the course of just two years, 480 airports, 78,000 bridges, and 40,000 public buildings were built.[354] The procurement of these assets served as stimulus for the broken economy and played a critical role in facilitating its recovery. They would lay the foundation for modern life in America.

It was infrastructure that breathed life back into a dying nation.

The New Deal was a revolutionary approach to fighting the depression. In the face of lost profits and economic uncertainty, the government refused to back into a corner. It adopted the radical stance that true recovery would require serious investment into the American people. The vehicle chosen was infrastructure, and it worked. Building projects brought jobs to local communities. Once operational, they facilitated the growth of business, connected people to markets, and massively expanded the availability of essential services.

In many ways, the coronavirus pandemic and its resulting economic crisis are similar to the conditions prevalent during the Great Depression. Unemployment has skyrocketed

---

353 Smith, *Building New Deal Liberalism*, 2.
354 Ibid.

across the world. Entire industries have been shut down due to social distancing measures, sending the world into its greatest recession since the dark days of the early 1930s. The International Monetary Fund has estimated a global GDP contraction of 4.4 percent. While the downturn isn't quite as large as the Great Depression, its effects have been similarly devastating.[355]

Developing countries have been hit particularly hard. Shahida Khatun is a young woman from Bangladesh whose family was sent back into the depths of poverty by the pandemic. As early as when she was twelve, Shahida began working in a garment factory instead of going to school. Though the work was difficult and went on for countless hours, the money she made brought her family a level of prosperity they had never experienced before. Because of her job, they were able to afford regular meals. After getting laid off in March of 2020, it was like going back right to where they started. Forced to go into debts with the local grocer just to secure enough for a single meal, chronic hunger has returned as an inescapable part of her life.[356]

"The garment factory helped me and my family to get out of poverty, but the coronavirus has pushed me back in," she told the *New York Times* in April of 2020.[357]

In the last two decades, Bangladesh has brought 20 percent of its population out of poverty. Now, with millions like

---

355 IMF, *World Economic Outlook*, 8.
356 Abi-Habib, "Millions."
357 Ibid.

Shahida losing their jobs, those developments are slowly being erased.[358] The United Nations estimated half a billion people could fall into some form of poverty as a result of the pandemic.[359] That's 8 percent of the total human population. In sub-Saharan Africa, half of all jobs were at risk of being temporarily (in some cases permanently) shut down.[360] The International Energy Agency predicted in 2020 that rates of electricity access in sub-Saharan Africa would decrease for the first time in six years.[361]

Abhijit Banerjee, professor at MIT and winner of the 2019 Nobel Prize in Economics said in April 2020, "There will be groups of people who climbed up the ladder and will now fall back. There were so many fragile existences, families barely stitching together an existence. They will fall back into poverty, and they may not come out of it."[362]

It's a stark message that points to the possibility of decades of progress being reversed. Yet, just as the Great Depression gave rise to the New Deal, the whole world is now faced with an opportunity to pursue an infrastructure-led recovery. Doing so will aid the recovery and development of the most affected countries in three important ways. First, filling urgent infrastructure gaps will help nations respond and adapt to the most immediate disruptions caused by the coronavirus. In particular, healthcare and hospital systems, telecommunications, and logistics have been identified as

---

358 Ibid.
359 Sumner, Hoy, and Ortiz-Juarez, *Estimates*.
360 Fox and Signé, "COVID-19."
361 IEA, *SDG7*.
362 Habib, "Millions."

paramount in the effort to fight the pandemic. Other forms of infrastructure will also be needed to address the impoverishing effects of the economic fallout, including remote learning capabilities for schools as well as water and sanitation. Initially, this will mostly require upgrading existing assets due to the difficult and long-term nature of building new ones.[363]

Second, development of new projects will help to accelerate economic recovery and bring jobs to sectors that have suffered particularly hard under COVID-19. Robust investments in infrastructure can revitalize the domestic and international demand. It can lead to greater investment by the private sector seeking to recover their business and strengthen supply chains.[364]

Finally, investing in infrastructure now presents the opportunity to build a more resilient and sustainable future. Jingdong Hua, vice president and treasurer of the World Bank said in July of 2020, "We need resilient, robust, green infrastructure, be it digital infrastructure or real infrastructure, from green energy to logistics. All of these elements are critical in the efforts after the pandemic to build resilient, sustainable economies and continue our trajectory in the United Nations and World Bank to end global poverty."[365]

The recovery from this pandemic will be long and painful, but a number of important lessons will be learned. Populations

---

363 Greenwood, "Asia's Infrastructure Imperative."
364 Ibid.
365 Hua, "Green Transition."

with access to dependable water and energy will be much better suited to weather the storm of future shocks. Economies bolstered by strong telecommunications and transportation networks will be prepared for swift adaptations like a transition to remote work. Sustainable infrastructure can be the key to ensuring a crisis of this scale never happens again.

FINDING THE MONEY, AGAIN

Rich developed countries were quick to roll out massive stimulus packages when the pandemic hit. By June of 2020, Western European nations had already allocated four trillion dollars of government spending to support their economies through the recession.[366] Of course, that money (and it is *a lot* of money) wasn't just sitting somewhere locked away in a government vault waiting to be spent. It had to be borrowed. In other words, citizens and commercial banks had to lend to their governments. Despite the additional risk associated with lending during a crisis, investors were practically begging to purchase these relatively safe securities.[367]

The other portion of the money came from the central banks. The Federal Reserve, the European Central Bank, the Bank of Japan, and many other central banks in OECD countries stepped up to provide trillions of dollars' worth of liquidity. They did this by purchasing government bonds from commercial banks. This helped to keep interest rates low, allowing governments to borrow money at cheap rates well below one percent. Something similar happened during World

---

366 Cassim, "The $10 Trillion Rescue."
367 Inman, "Global Investors."

War II, when the Federal Reserve pledged to keep interest rates low throughout the duration of the war to support the military effort. Altogether, the actions of the governments and central banks of developed countries helped to ease the transition into a COVID-19-affected economy.[368]

Developing countries have not fared quite as well. Most lacked the institutional capacity to respond to the crisis. From low-quality healthcare systems to the lack of digital bandwidth and remote networks necessary for e-commerce and logistics, poor countries were hit hard and fast. The governments in these countries also sought to bolster their populations and economies through public spending, but many didn't have the kind of borrowing power necessary to roll out stimulus packages. The American government has access to essentially unlimited credit because it has the right to tax the wealthiest economy on the planet. The same is true of other developed countries, albeit to a lesser extent, but it's still sufficient enough to provide stimulus. Japan, for example, has a much easier time reaching out to the capital markets and borrowing money at cheap rates than Nigeria. Investors simply do not have the confidence to move their money into what they perceive as riskier assets. So, when it came to the coronavirus pandemic and the recession, developing countries were left out to dry.[369]

Adding to poor credit quality was the already ballooning amount of debt held by developing countries. In 2019, the total external debt of the seventy-three poorest countries

---

368 Smith and Goldstein, "$2,000,000,000,000."
369 UN/DESA, "Policy Brief."

in the world rose 9.5 percent to a record level of $744 billion from the year before.[370] When the pandemic hit, hundreds of billions of dollars' worth of remittances and foreign exchange revenues vanished, particularly in countries dependent on commodity exports or tourism.[371] The ability of these countries to service their debt through and beyond the COVID-19 crisis has become a huge cause for concern. As credit markets have tightened up and investors have sought refuge in safer assets, developing countries have also lost their ability to refinance their loans. By May of 2020, non-resident capital outflows from these nations had already reached nearly one hundred billion dollars.[372]

Over one hundred countries requested emergency financing from the International Monetary Fund. Defaults would mean years of lengthy and painful negotiations with potentially unforgiving creditors. Given the way that healthcare, education, and infrastructure is currently financed, unsustainable levels of public debt would be devastating for the future of development. Countries are on the precipice of falling into the deepest fiscal trap in history.[373]

As United Nations Secretary General António Guterres warned, "A situation in which a series of countries in insolvency might trigger a global depression."[374]

---

370 World Bank, *International Debt Statistics 2021*, 15.
371 UN/DESA, "Policy Brief."
372 Ibid.
373 Shalal and Lawder, "IMF Chief Economist."
374 Chilkoti and Steinhauser, "Covid's Next."

Developing countries are in a double bind. On one hand, they need to incorporate the lessons of the Marshall Plan and the New Deal and take an active, infrastructure-focused approach to recovering from the COVID-19 crisis. On the other hand, rising levels of debt are preventing them from accessing the kind of money they need, and large interest payments are eating away at public coffers. For example, Zambian government debt surpassed 100 percent of its gross domestic product in 2020 due to a 5 percent contraction of its economy. At this rate, it will spend over a third of the entire government budget on debt service payments. The value of Zambia's currency, the kwacha, has also fallen dramatically, from five to the dollar to eighteen in 2020, making its debt levels over three times higher in local currency terms.[375]

THE CONSCIOUS MIND OF THE INVESTOR

The global infrastructure gap has been a thorn in the side of sustainable growth for some time now, but the imperative to close it has never been more important. We've reached a critical point where countries in desperate need of robust energy, water, transport, and telecommunications systems are more constrained than ever in their ability to pay for them. If there was ever a time to push forward with new, innovative ways to deliver sustainable infrastructure, it is now.

One way or another, countries have had to respond to the pandemic. The money they choose to spend during their paths to recovery will lay the foundation for growth and development for the next decades. The pandemic wasn't

---

375 Ibid.

the first crisis humanity has faced, and it won't be the last. Depending on the decisions we make today, our world could either emerge from this crisis just as vulnerable as before, or it could invest in a more promising, resilient, and sustainable future for us all. If stimulus spending and private investments can target sectors promoting the Sustainable Development Goals, this pandemic could be the very wake-up call the world needs to retire a global economic system that has been so wasteful and unequal for so long.

Many of the barriers to achieving the SDGs are well known. As the world moves forward beyond the pandemic, a new global agenda dedicated to seriously removing these barriers will be paramount. The relationships between local and national governments, international institutions, and the private sector will have to be reexamined and restructured to create conditions that are more conducive to this agenda. More importantly, there needs to be a radical shift in the way investors understand global crises and their role in the building resilience, particularly with regards to climate change.

As Vice President and Treasurer of the World Bank Jingdong Hua said, "Our journey is working with international capital markets to put sustainability into the conscious mind of investors."[376]

Global investors and policymakers have to wake up to the opportunity represented by investments in sustainability. They have to understand the economic consequences of *not* investing in climate resilience will be far more devastating

---

[376] Hua, "Green Transition."

than whatever short-term losses they may incur by reallocating their assets. Unfortunately, climate concern at both public and private levels has not translated into the kind of tangible action that is needed. The global infrastructure gap is but one example of that. In spite of the world's shortcomings, I want to highlight two recent developments that give me hope for the future.

First, green and renewable infrastructure is now more viable than it has ever been. Every year, the International Energy Agency (IEA) publishes a new edition of its *World Energy Outlook*, a highly influential publication that guides energy policy across the world. A statement was made in the 2020 edition that cannot go unnoticed. Paraphrasing won't do it any justice. It read, "For projects with low-cost financing that tap high-quality resources, solar PV is now the cheapest source of electricity in history."[377]

Let that sink in.

It means the story of Scaling Solar in Zambia wasn't a fluke. It was the beginning of a revolution. As a result of technological advancements and supportive policies, solar power not only costs less than coal or gas in most countries, but it also now offers electricity at the cheapest rates ever seen. For example, utility-scale solar projects now cost anywhere from twenty to forty dollars per MWh in countries like India and China. In comparison, new coal-fired power plants can cost up to $120/MWh. The lower costs of renewables will make them a

---

377 IEA, *World Energy Outlook*.

far more attractive option for investors and energy providers all over the world.[378]

The IEA predicts renewable energy sources can be reasonably expected to meet up to 80 percent of the growth in electricity demand over the next decade. With globalization and urbanization mounting pressure on energy assets across the developing world, this is incredibly good news. All of the biggest economies today were built through fossil fuels. Now, with solar becoming the "new king of electricity," the developing economies of the world have access to a cheaper, more sustainable option.[379]

The second development that gives me hope comes from an open letter sent by Larry Fink, the CEO of BlackRock. As the world's largest multinational investment management corporation with nearly nine trillion dollars in assets under its control, BlackRock is one of the most powerful forces in finance. In every year since the global financial crisis, Fink has written and published his "Letter to CEOs," an open essay highlighting what he sees as the foremost issues facing the companies BlackRock is invested in. It's a letter heard and analyzed in every boardroom on every continent.[380]

In the 2021 edition of this letter, Fink focuses passionately on one particular issue: climate change. In his words, "I believe that the pandemic has presented such an existential crisis – such a stark reminder of our fragility – that it has driven us to

---

378 Bailey, "King Solar."
379 IEA, *World Energy Outlook*.
380 Fink, "2021 Letter to CEOs."

confront the global threat of climate change more forcefully and to consider how, like the pandemic, it will alter our lives... No issue ranks higher than climate change on our clients' lists of priorities. They ask us about it nearly every day."[381]

Fink warns of the effect that natural disasters and resource insecurity will have on future of the global economy. He calls for companies to take climate change seriously lest their businesses suffer the consequences. As climate risk becomes more and more apparent, those companies that fail to adapt will lose the faith of their investors in what he calls "a fundamental reallocation of capital." He sees a world in which unsustainability is penalized, both in the physical and financial world.[382]

But Fink's letter wasn't only about cautioning the risks posed by climate change, it was also an announcement of the *opportunity* it represents. He writes, "We know that climate risk is investment risk. But we also believe the climate transition presents a historic investment opportunity." In the eyes of BlackRock, addressing climate change through sustainability and resilience won't come as an additional cost to businesses and the economy, as delusional politicians bought out by the fossil fuel industry will try to claim. In fact, quite the opposite is true. Countries and companies that invest now to transform their economies will be massively rewarded for it.[383]

---

381 Ibid.
382 Ibid.
383 Ibid.

There is evidence in the capital markets to corroborate these claims. Over the course of the year 2020, investors in mutual funds and exchange-traded funds poured $288 billion into global sustainable assets, a 96 percent increase over the year before. BlackRock research also showed that companies with superior environmental, social, and governance (ESG) profiles consistently outperformed their peers throughout 2020. As Fink writes, "81% of a globally-representative selection of sustainable indexes outperformed their parent benchmarks."[384]

Fink concludes his letter by asking companies to honor the Paris Agreement goal of keeping global warming below two degrees Celsius and commit to achieving net zero emissions by the year 2050. He also includes a nod to the infrastructure gap and emphasizes collaboration between public and private sectors as a key to closing it, writing, "Governments around the world, under severe fiscal strain from the pandemic, also need to undertake massive climate infrastructure projects, both to protect against physical risk and to deliver clean energy. These challenges will require creative public-private partnership to finance them, as well as better disclosures to attract capital."[385]

Mind you, Fink's words are just that: words. Taking action will be the difficult part. Whether or not the world chooses to take the necessary steps to build sustainability and resilience is yet to be seen. Still, the significance of this letter cannot be overlooked. Companies have put out vague statements about

---

[384] Ibid.
[385] Ibid.

their values and the ethics behind their decisions for decades, but never in a manner this bold. Since its inception, capitalism has come at the expense of the environment, and climate change is the price we have to pay for it. For so long, the powers that be have been too rich or too ignorant to address this issue, the belief being that saving the environment would come at the cost of corporate profits. If Larry Fink is to be believed, none of that is true anymore. If he means what he says, then he is calling for a revolution, a transformation of the economy, the planet, and humanity itself. If the rest of the world can sign off on his statement, it may just be enough to avoid the worst of the world's next crisis.

There are a couple of reasons why I choose to believe Larry Fink's open letter was more than just a PR stunt. First, it comes in the wake of a pandemic and the worst economic crash since the Great Depression. One might have imagined that such a crisis would divert attention away from the climate issue, but the opposite has been true. A similar statement during times of prosperity may be more dubious, but the timing of this letter offers it a certain credibility.

Second, I don't believe BlackRock is trying to pretend to be something it is not. If an all-encompassing encyclopedia were to be written at the end of times, BlackRock's logo might have a good chance of appearing under the entry for "capitalism." The company is for-profit through and through. Its nine trillion dollars in assets under management is proof of it. If sustainability and climate resilience is what BlackRock truly believes to be the best investment opportunity moving forward, it has no reason to lie. Furthermore, the money BlackRock manages is primarily the savings of many millions of individuals and pension beneficiaries, not its own. In the very first paragraph of his open letter, Larry Fink acknowledges his company's role as a "fiduciary" to these clients and its responsibility to advocate on their behalf.[386]

Finally, I believe in Larry Fink's message because I believe it to be true. This entire book is a testament to that. Sustainable infrastructure will be a critical component of building resilience to climate change, conflict, and pandemics. Investors who understand this will not only play a role in building a more prosperous future for humanity, but they can also capitalize on the most important investment opportunity of their lifetimes. I believe this is the realization that BlackRock has come to.

Our world may be teetering on the edge of a climate crisis, but it is also preparing to change. Leaders at all levels of government will have to partner with the private sector to take advantage of the momentum toward sustainability seen in the year 2020. The decades ahead will be incredibly important. They will be difficult. Whether we fail or succeed, the world order as we know it will undergo a transformation the likes of which we have never seen. What that transformation looks like is completely up to us.

---

386 Ibid.

12

SWING FOR THE FENCES

What is the nature of your responsibility to the world?
—JIM YONG KIM

It's hard to narrow down any one inspiration I had for writing this book, but there is one story I heard that marked the very beginning of this journey. I'd like to tell that story now.

Over the course of his career, Dr. Jim Yong Kim has cemented himself as one of the biggest names in global development. If you take a quick glance at his LinkedIn profile, you'll find it sparsely populated with details about his background, but the mere logos of his past organizations speak for themselves, to say nothing of his over two million followers. Within just ten years, he would carry such titles as World Health Organization director, Harvard Medical School professor, Dartmouth College president, and, most notably, president of the World Bank.[387]

---

387 World Bank, "Jim Yong Kim."

Jim was born in Seoul, South Korea in 1959, when the country was still amongst the poorest in the world. At the age of five, his family immigrated to Iowa, where he was raised. His mother was a philosopher, and she raised him to understand and care about social justice at an early age. Since he was twelve, he would find himself listening to speeches from Martin Luther King Jr. and attending George McGovern rallies. His father, on the other hand, was a North Korean refugee who became a dentist. He was a practical man, to say the least. He wanted stability, above all, for his children. Having established himself within the white suburbs of Iowa through this profession, he had high hopes for his son to pursue a similar path. Jim, however, had other plans in mind.[388]

Their divergence in thinking came to a head one day as Jim's father was driving him home from his sophomore year in college.[389]

"Jim, what are your aspirations?" he asked, knowing full well what he wanted to hear.[390]

Jim had carried the spirit of his mother's convictions for the poor into his undergraduate years. He would spend his free time at Brown University at the Third World Center and stay up late at night debating about racial justice and identity politics with his friends.[391]

---

388 Kim, "Good Life."
389 Ibid.
390 Ibid.
391 Ibid.

He replied, "I'm going to study political science and philosophy, and I'm going to become a part of a political movement."[392]

Wrong answer. His father slowly pulled the car over to the side of the road, looked over at his son, and said, "You finish your medical residency, and you can study anything you want."

As a Korean refugee during a time when Asian representation was non-existent, Jim's father understood who his family was in the country. "You're a Chinaman," he would say. "Get a skill that nobody can take away from you."

This was, and, to an extent, still is a common sentiment amongst ethnic minorities. Becoming a lawyer, doctor, or engineer effectively prevented others from writing you off simply for the color of your skin.

So that's what Jim did. He enrolled at Harvard Medical School, but he refused to solely live out his father's dream. He never let go of his own aspirations. As a student pursuing dual degrees in medicine and anthropology, he dove even deeper into grand ideas of social justice, reading Marx, Habermas, and Braudel alongside his biology and chemistry textbooks.[393]

One snowy evening, Jim and his classmate, Paul Farmer, sat outside in the Harvard square, sipping coffee and wondering

---

392 Ibid.
393 Ibid.

for hours how they were going to bring social justice into the medical field. Jim would never forget that night, having come away with the question that was going to dictate the rest of his life.[394]

"What is the nature of our responsibility to the world?"[395]

Jim and Paul Farmer would go on to start Partners in Health, an organization that pioneered a revolutionary model of providing healthcare to the world's poor. They found themselves treating tuberculosis in the slums of Lima, Peru at a time when none of the global health leaders believed it could be done. On top of that, a new strain of TB had surfaced seemingly out of nowhere that was resistant to drugs. The World Health Organization's formal position at the time was that treating drug-resistant TB was simply not cost effective enough. It wasn't incorrect. The average cost to treat a single patient in the early 1990s was over $20,000. The Peruvian government itself decided to turn a blind eye. Nobody thought it was possible. Meanwhile, over 500,000 patients were falling deathly ill every year, the vast majority of whom were severely impoverished.[396]

But it wasn't enough for Jim and Partners in Health to give up. Letting these people die would go against every ounce of his being. It would ignore the compassion for others his mother had left him. Even as the international health community condemned them for what it perceived as arrogance, they

---

394 Kim, "Revolutionizing."
395 Ibid.
396 Harvey, "The Healer."

persevered in the fight to prove these patients deserved an equal chance at living a good life. Without much help, Jim and Paul began treating the people in Lima themselves. They called the program Socios En Salud and indebted themselves to purchase the necessary drugs out of their own pockets. It was the beginning of a global movement.[397]

Eventually, Jim was able to convince the WHO to add the necessary drugs for treating this disease to the list of essential medicines. That was the first step in creating a market for the wildly expensive drugs. As competition from generics manufacturers seeped in, the cost of the medications dropped 90 percent. Jim and his organization had won the battle. They proved it was not only possible to treat drug-resistant TB among the world's poor, but it was absolutely necessary. The program Partners in Health introduced has gone on to treat over 30,000 such cases all across the globe.[398]

Dr. Kim's guiding motive was never what was possible. It wasn't whatever was expedient. Instead, his actions were guided by an acknowledgment of his responsibility. What if it weren't? What if he had pursued the guaranteed path and achieved the financial stability his father sought for him? He certainly would have deserved it. But what would've become of those patients in the slums of Lima, Peru no one else was willing to treat? By recognizing the power of his education and using it without fear or bitterness, Jim was able to obtain something truly meaningful. He obtained a set of skills that

---

[397] Ibid.
[398] Ibid.

were irremovable and used them to honor the compassion for others his mother instilled in him.

Jim later became a director at the WHO, the very organization he fought against, to replicate his quest to treat drug-resistant diseases, this time for HIV. During his time in office, millions of HIV patients were treated in Africa. Had he followed the path of traditional medicine in the way his father intended, and undoubtedly as many of his classmates at Harvard and Brown did, this work, this lifesaving, transformational work would at best be left to someone else. For all his experience and expertise working in developing countries and pushing the envelope on what can be done for the poor, Dr. Kim was nominated by President Obama to become the twelfth president of the World Bank, a position never before been held by someone with a medical background.[399]

FINDING MYSELF IN DEVELOPMENT, AND DEVELOPMENT IN MYSELF

I don't know that I have a personal connection to emerging markets infrastructure, or even to global development in general. I tried to find one while writing this book (it would have made explaining to people why I was writing it a lot easier), but I couldn't. At least, not an obvious one. Both of my parents grew up poor in a developing country, but I didn't. I grew up middle-class in suburban Illinois. My parents succeeded in shielding me from the hardships they faced, so my childhood was filled with soccer practice, movie nights, and ski trips.

---

399 Ibid.

Growing up, I would ask my parents to tell me stories from their own childhoods. I remember being fascinated with what they did on special occasions like birthdays or the new year. It was only on those days when they could eat meat. Some years, my mom would be surprised by my grandfather with a small piece of hard candy or some baked sweet bread. She told me she would try to make the rare sugary treats last as long as possible by chewing slowly. That part always kind of stuck with me.

My dad grew up in the mountains, so his youth was full of adventures. He would tell me about swimming in wild rivers and voyaging through dense forests. Once a year, he would go by himself on a long journey on foot to the farm where his uncle raised hunting dogs. He would set off at the crack of dawn and arrive long after sundown, braving a harsh environment full of thorns and wild animals. His family was even poorer than my mom's, and for a number of reasons, he was separated from his father (my grandfather) at an early age. There was a sadness to those stories I didn't fully understand at the time. It played out in small ways, I think.

One of the greatest luxuries I had growing up was the option to be interested in many things. In high school, I fell in love with literature and philosophy. I was on the debate team, so I spent my time reading and talking about the works of authors like Karl Marx, John Rawls, and Amartya Sen. My mind was filled with ideas about social justice, oppression, and all the various issues facing marginalized groups. I spent several of my summers as a teenager campaigning for local candidates who championed causes I believed in. Because of the Internet, I had innumerable resources at my disposal to immerse myself in these topics and develop an awareness of what was happening in the world around me.

But there was something else I was chasing at the same time, a force as powerful as passion in driving my actions: excellence. I wanted to do justice to the life my parents worked so hard to give me. I wanted to exceed expectations. I wanted to perform well relative to my peers. I wanted to be a winner. Luckily for me, the things I was interested in and the things I wanted to succeed at went hand in hand. I wasn't alone in these types of endeavors. Many of my closest friends in high school were similarly involved in causes for the less fortunate. They spent countless hours mentoring underprivileged kids, volunteering in hospitals, and protesting in political rallies, striving at the same time to make their parents proud and set themselves up for future success.

I started off my first year of college in 2018 at Vanderbilt University. One of the things that happens when you leave your hometown for the first time is people start asking you where that hometown is. I didn't like answering that question at first. Admittedly, despite the comforts of my upbringing, I felt slightly ashamed about where I came from. I was as much of a suburbanite as anyone could possibly be, albeit from an immigrant family, but my midwestern-ness was fully represented every time I said the words "Palatine, Illinois." I didn't think it was interesting compared to the people I met who were from multicultural hubs like New York City and Dallas or from faraway countries like the Netherlands or Zimbabwe. Nashville itself was one of the hottest up-and-coming metropolitan destinations, and the place itself became a standard I wanted to live up to. I got away for a time with saying I was from Chicago, but there were enough students from the suburban Chicagoland area for others to sniff out the truth.

Drawing from some of my favorite courses and topics in high school, I chose economics and sociology as the two disciplines I would focus my studies on. I had a feeling I might be interested in global development, though I hadn't immersed myself in the subject yet. But something else that happens in college is people start caring less about what you're interested in and more about what you'll do after graduation.

"What are you planning on doing with that degree?"

I don't necessarily disagree with that question. It really comes down to preparing for the future, which is part of the reason why higher education exists, but there were a number of pressures related to it I had never felt before. I started to make decisions that were consciously and unconsciously motivated by those pressures. Excellence, as it turned out, had a different definition when it came to jobs and occupations. Money and stability were now a part of the equation. Even more potent was the social pressure. I wanted the career paths other students wanted.

Two of the organizations I first joined as a freshman in college were the consulting club and the investment club. They were meant to educate and help students looking to find careers in management consulting or finance. Truthfully, I didn't care much for either option, and I couldn't give you a reason as to why I stayed in those clubs. Thankfully, no one ever seemed too keen on asking. Wanting to work in finance was as normal for students as wearing a backpack on campus.

As I dove deeper into this world of future careers, my school became less of the apex of intellectual curiosity I had romanticized it to be and more of a steppingstone into corporate life. I was going through a feeder system for big companies signing big paychecks. I found myself standing in the longest lines at career fairs without really thinking twice about it. Companies would arrive on campus to scout out freshman talent before they even declared their majors. I was bombarded with emails from corporate recruiters peddling opportunities to meet their teams and apply to their internships.

College kids are addicted to many things, and prestige is not the least among them. In the same way I vied for admission to a high-ranking university, I found myself competing voraciously for jobs and internships. The allures of exclusivity, social standing, and a large salary were incredibly tempting to me, and companies seemed all too eager for me to take a stab at their selective summer opportunities. I started coming up with creative excuses as to why my academic interests led to such decisions.

I once heard an art history major from Columbia explain why her love of nineteenth century impressionist paintings made her interested in investment banking because reading financial statements was like finding the stories hidden in artwork. Seriously.

For the most part, I kept my course load separate from these new activities. My appetite for the social sciences, philosophy, and development economics hadn't abated, and I reveled in the knowledge of my professors and the university's endless resources. I reached a place where my time was divided between two pursuits that were completely intellectually unrelated, one that satisfied my immediate curiosities and one that would land me a fancy job.

During one semester, I was enrolled in four courses titled Environment and Development, Poverty and Discrimination, Latin American Development, and The Sociology of Green Jobs. When I wasn't working on course materials, I would study financial statements and prepare for technical finance interviews. I would go from writing an essay about corporate gluttony and the disastrous greed of Wall Street directly to writing a cover letter about why I wanted to be a banker. To be clear, I don't hold anything against corporate careers like investment banking or consulting or any of the people who go into those jobs. They are great career options and are attractive for valid reasons. I personally desired them for reasons I couldn't justify to myself.

Inexplicably, it was the corporate side of me I felt more comfortable sharing with others. I didn't have to explain it as much. Working some glamorous investment banking or consulting job felt more fitting of my background and the person I was becoming. The funny thing is, I never experienced any direct pressures from my parents or my peers to pursue a certain type of career. My parents were always supportive of everything I wanted to do and anything I was interested in. They made it a point to remind me they would approve of any career path I chose for myself. It was a luxury they didn't have.

Both of my parents studied environmental engineering as undergraduate and master's students. They were preparing to work on issues like water efficiency and sustainability in local Chinese municipalities. My dad spent his post-graduate years training with international NGOs on sustainability issues in Sweden. But right before my older brother was born, the opportunity arose for my dad to get a computer science degree and work as a software engineer in the United States. It wasn't something he could pass up on. It meant a kind of prosperity generations upon generations of his family had never experienced before. Because China's one child policy was still enforced at that time, it literally meant the difference between me existing and never being born.

But even with the freedom they afforded me, I still couldn't bring myself to tell them what I truly wanted out of my life. Quietly, I was spending my time buried in scholarly literature and podcasts produced by anti-poverty camps across the globe. I had the words of Jeffrey Sachs and Paul Collier playing through my headphones every waking moment. I listened to every single public interview and speech given by Dr. Jim Yong Kim several times over. I became deeply, deeply fascinated with the problem of the infrastructure gap and how it might be closed. But I didn't tell a soul.

My cognitive dissonance came to a head when I heard Dr. Kim tell the story at the beginning of this chapter for the first time. I'm not bold enough to say I identify with the strength of his character or his conviction for the poor, but his story and his message about responsibility resonated deeply inside of me. What was the nature of my responsibility to the world?

For Dr. Kim, the answer to that question was in the slums of Lima, Peru.

What was my responsibility to the world? Did I truly think a six-figure corporate job was going to allow me to have the kind of impact I wanted to make? Who told me that? I couldn't get those questions out of my head. Given the education I was receiving and the set of opportunities I was privileged enough to have, the answer was clearly not in corporate finance or consulting.

I had to find a way out.

I don't know what it's like to grow up in a developing country. I don't know what's it's like to live life without infrastructure. My access to water, energy, transport, and telecommunications has not been threatened by climate change, pandemics, violent conflict, overpopulation, starvation, inequality, or extreme poverty. I struggle to think I should have the audacity to imagine myself as the right person to tackle these issues. I have nothing yet on my resume that qualifies me, no accomplishment or good deed I can point to that has left a lasting mark in the countries I'm writing about.

Upon embarking on this journey, I believed I had no connection to any of these things I care so deeply about. But neither did I have a connection to any of the corporations or career paths that diverted my attentions. Upon realizing this, I also realized the first statement was never true. My connection is the thoughts that occupy my head. It's the news I pay attention to, the books I read, and the people I admire. My connection is the fact I *know* what's happening in the darkest corners of the world, despite never having the misfortune of *feeling* it. My connection is the fact that all living, breathing humans share the same earth and that none of the greatest challenges we now face can be solved without the work of us all. And that connection, after reading these pages, is now yours too.

There will be countless moments in your life where you will see yourself as the wrong person to do something, even if that something is important to you. At the same time, you will know exactly how everyone else on this planet lives. You'll be aware of the struggles they go through. It's all one tap of a button away. What should you do with your opportunity? What kind of responsibility comes with the life that you live?

SWING FOR THE FENCES

There's a saying commonly used in the sport of baseball. *Swing for the fences.* It refers to when the batter steps up to the plate and swings at the ball as hard as they possibly can. It means they are putting the fate of the entire game on the line, perhaps at the expense of precision and accuracy. But there's no other choice. All hopes and aspirations for victory are channeled into that one swing.

Our world is on the precipice of disaster. In many ways, disaster is already here. You can see it in the natural disasters that rage through South Asia, in the violence and despair growing rampant in the Middle East and North Africa, and in the desertification of Sub-Saharan Africa. There are no challenges greater than the ones we face today. But there is hope on the horizon. Sustainable infrastructure can be an instrument of change the likes of which we have never before seen. Resilience and prosperity can be built in the most vulnerable places of the world.

It won't be easy. Trillions of dollars stand in our way. Institutional weakness and instability jeopardize investments that can save lives. Private negligence of these global challenges prevents us from cooperating on much-needed solutions. Selfishness and unwillingness to put aside our differences and work together are putting billions in jeopardy.

But the money is there. The people passionate and desperate are there. The problem can be solved. The ball is in our court. The cards are in our hands. We'll have to swing for the fences. It's time for this world to come together, use the resources at our disposal, and take responsibility for our shared prosperity. If we do, the rest of the twenty-first century might very well be characterized by the end of massive and preventable suffering amongst those caged by vulnerability. We will have the chance to grow equitably and fairly in a safer and more inclusive world. It's time to close the global infrastructure gap.

ACKNOWLEDGMENTS

My sincerest gratitude for all the kindness and generosity given to me from all my supporters, without whom this work would never have possible.

Abhi Balu
Angie Peng
Alan Tang
Aleena Boby
Ashwin West
Audrey Pope
Baojun Zhang
Baraa Alkhani
Colin Walsh
Daniel Mativo
Davis Kornblum
Drake Schaub
Ed Li
Eric Koester
Eugene Kim
Georg Inderst
Grace Liu

Guolong Li
Jackie Dickens
James Geist
Jeffery Liao
Jiang Kun
Joy Tang
Kannan Lakmeeharan
Kashif Javid
Kyle Birmingham
Lauren Mauresca
Lei Ning
Lijun Chen
Lu Yang
Mattigan Kelly
Michael Chen
Michael Wang
Patrick Ruan
Rachel Wei
Rajiv Sharma
Raffaele Della Croce
Romina Bandura
Sanagami Pugazenthi
Shannon Shen
Shrikant Avi
Sterling Gilliam
Tomás Serebrisky
Xia Chen
Xiujuan He
Weining Cui
Yi Ruan
Yonggang Ruan

APPENDIX

INTRODUCTION

Bhattacharya, Amar, Joshua P. Meltzer, Jeremy Oppenheim, and Nicholas Stern. *Delivering on Sustainable Infrastructure for Better Development and Better Climate.* Washington DC: Brookings Institution, 2016. https://www.brookings.edu/wp-content/uploads/2016/12/global_122316_delivering-on-sustainable-infrastructure.pdf.

ESMAP. *Maximizing Finance for Development in Egypt's Energy Sector.* Washington, DC: World Bank, 2019. http://documents1.worldbank.org/curated/en/780061567532224696/pdf/Maximizing-Finance-for-Development-in-Egypts-Energy-Sector.pdf.

Global Infrastructure Hub. *Global Infrastructure Outlook.* Sydney: Global Infrastructure Hub, 2017. https://outlook.gihub.org/.

Hussain, Ali Abid, Selim Jeddi, Kannan Lakmeeharan, and Hasan Muzaffar. "Unlocking Private-Sector Financing in Emerging-Markets Infrastructure." *McKinsey & Company*, October 10, 2019. https://www.mckinsey.com/industries/private-equity-and-principal-investors/our-insights/unlocking-private-sector-financing-in-emerging-markets-infrastructure.

International Energy Agency. *SDG7: Data and Projections*. Paris: IEA, 2020. https://www.iea.org/reports/sdg7-data-and-projections.

Inter-American Development Bank. *What is Sustainable Infrastructure? A Framework to Guide Sustainability Across the Project Cycle*. Washington, DC: Inter-American Development Bank, 2018. https://publications.iadb.org/publications/english/document/What_is_Sustainable_Infrastructure__A_Framework_to_Guide_Sustainability_Across_the_Project_Cycle.pdf.

International Labor Organization. *ILO Monitor: COVID-19 and the World of Work. Seventh Edition. Updated Estimates and Analysis*. Geneva: International Labor Organization, 2021.

Kelley, Colin P., Shahrzad Mohtadi, Mark A. Cane, Richard Seager, Yochanan Kushnir. "Climate Change in the Fertile Crescent and Implications of the Recent Syrian Drought." *Proceedings of the National Academy of Sciences* 112, no.11 (2015): 3241-3246. https://doi.org/10.1073/pnas.1421533112.

Kim, Jim Yong. "Human Capital and Technology: Building the New Social Contract." Speech, Stanford University, October 2, 2018. World Bank. https://www.worldbank.org/en/news/speech/2018/10/02/pre-annual-meetings-positioning-speech

Kingsley, Patrick. "Egypt Suffers Regular Blackouts Due to Worst Energy Crisis in Decades." *The Guardian*, August

20, 2014. https://www.theguardian.com/world/2014/aug/20/egypt-blackouts-energy-crisis-power-cuts.

Lakner, Christoph, Nishant Yonzan, Daniel Gerszon Mahler, R. Andres Castaneda Aguilar, and Haoyu Wu. "Updated Estimates of the Impact of COVID-19 on Global Poverty: Looking Back at 2020 and the Outlook for 2021." *Data Blog. World Bank*, January 11, 2021.

Lewis, Aidan. "Giant Solar Park in the Desert Jump Starts Egypt's Renewables Push." *Reuters*, December 17, 2019. https://www.reuters.com/article/us-egypt-solar/giant-solar-park-in-the-desert-jump-starts-egypts-renewables-push-idUSKBN1YL1WS.

OECD/The World Bank/UN Environment, *Financing Climate Futures*. Paris: OECD Publishing, 2018. https://doi.org/10.1787/9789264308114-en.

Roser, Max, Esteban Ortiz-Ospina and Hannah Ritchie. "Life Expectancy." *OurWorldInData.org*, Last modified October 2019. https://ourworldindata.org/life-expectancy.

Schoch, Marta, and Christoph Lakner. "African Countries Show Mixed Progress Towards Poverty Reduction and Half of Them Have an Extreme Poverty Rate above 35%." *Data Blog. World Bank*, December 22, 2020. https://blogs.worldbank.org/opendata/african-countries-show-mixed-progress-towards-poverty-reduction-and-half-them-have-extreme.

Schwartztein, Peter. "Can Egypt's Crisis Help Clean Energy Gain Traction?" *National Geographic,* October 2, 2014. https://www.

nationalgeographic.com/science/article/141003-egypt-renewable-energy.

Selormey, Edem E., and Carolyn Logan. "African Nations Are among Those Most Vulnerable to Climate Change. a New Survey Suggests They Are Also the Least Prepared." *Washington Post*, September 23, 2019. https://www.washingtonpost.com/politics/2019/09/23/african-nations-are-among-those-most-vulnerable-climate-change-new-survey-suggests-they-are-also-least-prepared/.

Thacker S, Adshead D, Morgan G, Crosskey S, Bajpai A, Ceppi P, Hall JW and O'Regan N. *Infrastructure: Underpinning Sustainable Development*. Copenhagen: UNOPS, 2018. https://unops.economist.com/wp-content/uploads/2019/01/Infrastructure_underpining_sustainable_development_EN.pdf.

UNHCR. "Needs Soar as Number of Syrian Refugees Tops 3 Million." The United Nations High Commission for Refugees news release, August 29, 2014. UNCHR website. https://www.unhcr.org/53ff76c99.html, accessed December 12, 2020.

United Nations. "World's Least Developed Countries on Target to Achieve Universal and Affordable Internet by 2020." United Nations press release, January 24, 2018. UN website. https://www.un.org/ohrlls/news/world%E2%80%99s-least-developed-countries-target-achieve-universal-and-affordable-internet-2020, accessed August 25, 2020.

UNICEF/WHO. *Progress on Household Drinking Water, Sanitation, and Hygiene: Special Focus on Inequalities*. New York: United Nations Children's Fund (UNICEF) and World Health Organization, 2019. https://www.who.int/water_sanitation_health/publications/jmp-2019-full-report.pdf.

World Bank. "Egypt's Extra Electricity to Power More than Five Million Households." World Bank feature story, December 10, 2015. World Bank website. https://www.worldbank.org/en/news/feature/2015/12/17/egypts-extra-electricity-to-power-more-than-five-million-households, accessed June 30, 2020.

World Bank. *Poverty and Shared Prosperity 2020: Reversals of Fortune*. Washington, DC: World Bank, 2020.

CHAPTER 1

Amnesty International. "The Occupation of Water." Campaigns, November 29, 2017, Accessed December 15, 2020. https://www.amnesty.org/en/latest/campaigns/2017/11/the-occupation-of-water/.

charitywater. "The Journey Episode 2: Life without Clean Water." August 9, 2016. Video, 6:39. https://www.youtube.com/watch?v=yPxMOzNoUq4&ab_channel=charitywater.

Fantini, Christina, and Geoffrey Morgan. "Conflict, Climate Change and Infrastructure." UNOPS, November 27, 2020. UNOPS website. https://www.unops.org/news-and-stories/insights/conflict-climate-change-and-infrastructure.

Hickel, Jason. "Could You Live on $1.90 a Day? That's the International Poverty Line." *The Guardian*, November 1, 2015. https://www.theguardian.com/global-development-professionals-network/2015/nov/01/global-poverty-is-worse-than-you-think-could-you-live-on-190-a-day.

International Energy Agency. *SDG7: Data and Projections.* Paris: IEA, 2020. https://www.iea.org/reports/sdg7-data-and-projections.

Mahr, Krista. "Rahul Gandhi's Buzz: Indian Scion Offers Many Metaphors but Few Solutions." *Time,* April 05, 2013. https://world.time.com/2013/04/05/rahul-gandhis-buzz-indian-scion-offers-many-metaphors-but-few-solutions/.

Marques, Clara Ferreira. "China Scores Big against Poverty but the Poor Haven't Gone Away." *Bloomberg,* November 28, 2020. https://www.bloomberg.com/opinion/articles/2020-11-29/xi-jinping-scores-big-against-extreme-poverty-but-china-still-has-its-poor.

OECD, *Climate-Resilient Infrastructure.* Paris: OECD Publishing, 2018. http://www.oecd.org/environment/cc/policy-perspectives-climate-resilient-infrastructure.pdf.

Roser, Max, and Esteban Ortiz-Ospina. "Global Extreme Poverty." *OurWorldInData.org*, Last modified October 2019. https://ourworldindata.org/extreme-poverty.

Roser, Max, and Hannah Ritchie. "Clean Water." *OurWorldInData.org*, Last modified September 2019. https://ourworldindata.org/water-access.

Schoch, Marta, Christoph Lakner, and Samuel Frieje-Rodriguez. "Monitoring Poverty at the US$3.20 and US$5.50 Lines: Differences and Similarities with Extreme Poverty Trends." *Data Blog. World Bank*, November 19, 2020. https://blogs.worldbank.org/opendata/monitoring-poverty-us320-and-us550-lines-differences-and-similarities-extreme-poverty.

UNICEF/WHO. *Progress on Household Drinking Water, Sanitation, and Hygiene: Special Focus on Inequalities.* New York: United Nations Children's Fund (UNICEF) and World Health Organization, 2019. https://www.who.int/water_sanitation_health/publications/jmp-2019-full-report.pdf.

Weil Sydney. "How Does Water Use in the United States Compare to That in Africa?" *African Wildlife Foundation*, August 03, 2013. https://www.awf.org/blog/how-does-water-use-united-states-compare-africa.

World Bank. "Decline of Global Extreme Poverty Continues but Has Slowed: World Bank." World Bank press release, September 19, 2018. World Bank website. https://www.worldbank.org/en/news/press-release/2018/09/19/decline-of-global-extreme-poverty-continues-but-has-slowed-world-bank.

World Bank. "FAQs: Global Poverty Line Update." Understanding Poverty, September 30, 2015, Accessed December 15, 2020. https://www.worldbank.org/en/topic/poverty/brief/global-poverty-line-faq.

World Health Organization and United Nations Children's Fund Joint Monitoring Programme for Water Supply and Sanitation (JMP). *Progress on Drinking Water and Sanitation: Special Focus on Sanitation.* Geneva: WHO, 2008. https://www.who.int/water_sanitation_health/monitoring/jmp2008.pdf.

World Bank. *Poverty and Shared Prosperity 2018: Piecing Together the Poverty Puzzle.* Washington, DC: World Bank, 2018.

World Bank. *Poverty and Shared Prosperity 2020: Reversals of Fortune.* Washington, DC: World Bank, 2020.

CHAPTER 2

Bazi, Vincent, and M. Nicholas J. Firzli. "Infrastructure Investments in the Age of Austerity." *Revue Analyse Financiere,* no. 41 (2011): 34-37. http://nebula.wsimg.com/5b-d39c809b17edb595bcef072b5621e1?AccessKeyId=9BB168F-4CFBA64F592DA&disposition=0&alloworigin=1.

Bhattacharya, Amar, Joshua P. Meltzer, Jeremy Oppenheim, and Nicholas Stern. *Delivering on Sustainable Infrastructure for Better Development and Better Climate.* Washington DC: Brookings Institution, 2016. https://www.brookings.edu/wp-content/uploads/2016/12/global_122316_delivering-on-sustainable-infrastructure.pdf.

Biden, Joe (@JoeBiden). "President Trump campaigned on repairing our nation's crumbling infrastructure. But after countless "Infrastructure Weeks," he has failed to deliver results. It has to change. Today, I'm calling for a transformational investment in our nation's future." *Twitter,* November 14, 2019. https://twitter.com/JoeBiden/status/1194994646448922624.

Chang, Ha-Joon. *The East Asian Development Experience: The Miracle, the Crisis and the Future.* London: Zed Books, 2006.

Commission on Growth and Development. *The Growth Report: Strategies for Sustained Growth and Inclusive Development.* Washington, DC: World bank, 2008. https://openknowledge.worldbank.org/handle/10986/6507.

Garemo, Nicklas, Martin Hjerpe, and Brendan Halleman. *A Better Road to the Future: Improving the Delivery of Road Infrastructure across the World.* McKinsey & Company, 2018. https://www.mckinsey.com/~/media/mckinsey/industries/capital%20projects%20and%20infrastructure/our%20insights/improving%20the%20delivery%20of%20road%20infrastructure%20across%20the%20world/a-better-road-to-the-future-web-final.ashx#:~:text=McKinsey%20Global%20Institute%20(MGI)estimates,GDP%20in%20the%20long%20run.

Hajjar, Bandar. "The Children's Continent: Keeping up with Africa's Growth." *World Economic Forum*, January 13, 2020. https://www.weforum.org/agenda/2020/01/the-children-s-continent/.

International Bank for Reconstruction and Development, *The East Asian Miracle: Economic Growth and Public Policy.* Oxford: Oxford University Press, 1993.

Korea.net. "The Korean Economy – the Miracle on the Hangang River." Accessed September 12, 2020. https://www.korea.net/AboutKorea/Economy/The-Miracle-on-The-Hangang.

Kuddus, M.A., Elizabeth Tynan, and Emma McBryde. "Urbanization: A Problem for the Rich and the Poor?" *Public Health Rev* 41, no.1 (2020). https://doi.org/10.1186/s40985-019-0116-0.

Malthus, Thomas Robert. *An Essay on the Principle of Population; or, A View of Its past and Present Effects on Human Happiness.* London: Ward, Lock, and Company, 1890. https://www.google.com/books/edition/An_Essay_on_the_Principle_of_Population/38JJAQAAMAAJ?hl=en&gbpv=1.

OECD/The World Bank/UN Environment, *Financing Climate Futures*. Paris: OECD Publishing, 2018. https://doi.org/10.1787/9789264308114-en.

The Economist. "Africa's Population Will Double by 2050." *The Economist*, May 28, 2020. https://www.economist.com/special-report/2020/03/26/africas-population-will-double-by-2050.

UN Environment. *Global Environment Outlook – GEO-6: Healthy Planet, Healthy People.* Nairobi: UN Environment, 2019. https://10.1017/9781108627146.

United Nations. "Urbanization: Expanding Opportunities, but Deeper Divides." United Nations news release, August 29, 2014. United Nations website. https://www.un.org/development/desa/en/news/social/urbanization-expanding-opportunities-but-deeper-divides.html, accessed February 11, 2021.

Walker, Ruth. "Digging for 'Infrastructure' in the OED." *Christian Science Monitor*, November 20, 2013. https://www.csmonitor.com/The-Culture/Verbal-Energy/2013/1120/Digging-for-infrastructure-in-the-OED.

WIDER, UNU. *A Snapshot Of Poverty And Inequality In Asia: Experience Over The Last Fifty Years.* WIDER Research Brief

2020/2, Helsinki: UNU-WIDER, 2020. https://www.wider.unu.edu/publication/snapshot-poverty-and-inequality-asia.

Woetzel, Jonathan, Nicklas Garemo, Jan Mischke, and Brendan Halleman. *Bridging Global Infrastructure Gaps.* McKinsey Global Institute, 2018. https://www.mckinsey.com/business-functions/operations/our-insights/bridging-global-infrastructure-gaps.

Zanona, Melanie. "Trump: Nation's Infrastructure Can Be Fixed 'Only by Me'." *The Hill,* June 22, 2016. https://thehill.com/policy/transportation/284532-trump-nations-infrastructure-can-be-fixed-only-by-me.

CHAPTER 3

Ahmad, Latief, Raihana Habib Kanth, Sabah Parvaze, and Syed Sheraz Mahdi. *Experimental Agrometeorology: A Practical Manual.* Berlin: Springer, 2017.

Akpan, Nsikan. "Only 2 Countries Are Meeting Their Climate Pledges. Here's How the 10 Worst Could Improve." *PBS News Hour,* September 26, 2019. https://www.pbs.org/newshour/science/only-2-countries-are-meeting-their-climate-pledges-heres-how-the-10-worst-could-improve.

Anyadike, Obi. "Drought in Africa Leaves 45 Million in Need across 14 Countries." *The New Humanitarian,* June 10, 2019. https://www.thenewhumanitarian.org/analysis/2019/06/10/drought-africa-2019-45-million-in-need.

Banerji, Annie. "Bengaluru Water Crisis: More Work, Less Water in India's 'Silicon Valley'." *Mint*, June 05, 2019. https://www.livemint.com/news/india/bengaluru-water-crisis-more-work-less-water-in-india-s-silicon-valley-1559718058529.html.

Bhaumik, Subir. "India: 'World's Wettest Place' Suffers Water Shortage." *Al Jazeera*, January 5, 2016. https://www.aljazeera.com/features/2016/01/05/india-worlds-wettest-place-suffers-water-shortage/.

Boseley, Sarah. "World Bank to Name and Shame Countries That Fail to Prevent Stunting in Children." *The Guardian*, September 30, 2016. https://www.theguardian.com/global-development/2016/sep/30/world-bank-name-and-shame-countries-fail-stunted-children.

Chandler, David L. "Deadly Heat Waves Could Hit South Asia This Century." *MIT News Office*, August 02, 2017. https://news.mit.edu/2017/deadly-heat-waves-could-hit-south-asia-century-0802#:~:text=At%20a%20wet%2Dbulb%20temperature,31%20C%20anywhere%20on%20Earth.

CNA Insider. "Flooded by Climate Change: Will India Sink Or Swim? | Insight | Full Episode." September 30, 2020. Video, 47:38. https://www.youtube.com/watch?v=wyrpV5msbZ-k&t=199s&ab_channel=CNAInsider.

Denton, Bryan, and Somini Sengupta. "India's Ominous Future: Too Little Water, or Far Too Much." *New York Times*, November 25, 2019. https://www.nytimes.com/interactive/2019/11/25/climate/india-monsoon-drought.html.

Drainage Services Department. "Sponge City: Adapting to Climate Change." Accessed February 2, 2020. https://www.dsd.gov.hk/Documents/SustainabilityReports/1617/en/sponge_city.html.

Fountain, Henry. "Climate Change Is Accelerating, Bringing World 'Dangerously Close' to Irreversible Change." *New York Times*, June 13, 2019. https://www.nytimes.com/2019/06/13/world/asia/india-heat-wave-deaths.html.

Hu, Xi, Jim W. Hall, Peijun Shi, and Wee Ho Lim. "The Spatial Exposure of the Chinese Infrastructure System to Flooding and Drought Hazards." *Natural Hazards* 80, (2016): 1083-1119. https://doi.org/10.1007/s11069-015-2012-3.

Im, Eun-Soon, Jeremy S. Pal, and Elfatih A. B. Eltahir. "Deadly Heat Waves Projected in the Densely Populated Agricultural Regions of South Asia." *Science Advances* 3, no. 8 (2017. https://doi.org/10.1126/sciadv.1603322.

Javaheri, Pedram, and Michael Guy. "Historic End for India's Monsoon Season." *CNN*, October 6, 2020. https://www.cnn.com/2020/10/06/weather/india-monsoon-ends-historic-rainfall/index.html.

Kumar-Rao, Arati. "India's Water Crisis Could Be Helped by Better Building, Planning." *National Geographic*, July 25, 2019. https://www.nationalgeographic.com/environment/article/india-water-crisis-drought-could-be-helped-better-building-planning#close.

Mani, Muthukumara, Sushenjit Bandyopadhyay, Shun Chonabayashi, Anil Markandya, Thomas Mosier. *South Asia's Hotspots:*

The Impact of Temperature and Precipitation Changes on Living Standards. Washington, DC: World Bank, 2020. https://doi.org/10.1596/978-1-4648-1155-5.

Mashal, Mujib. "India Heat Wave, Soaring Up to 123 Degrees, Has Killed at Least 36." *New York Times*, June 13, 2019. https://www.nytimes.com/2019/06/13/world/asia/india-heat-wave-deaths.html.

NASA. "Global Temperature." Accessed January 5, 2020. https://climate.nasa.gov/vital-signs/global-temperature/#:~:text=Nineteen%20of%20the%20warmest%20years,source%3A%20NASA%2FGISS).

OECD, *Climate-Resilient Infrastructure*. Paris: OECD Publishing, 2018. http://www.oecd.org/environment/cc/policy-perspectives-climate-resilient-infrastructure.pdf.

Pai, D.S., Latha Sridhar, M.R. Badwaik, and M. Rajaveen. "Analysis of the Daily Rainfall Events over India Using a New Long Period (1901–2010) High Resolution (0.25° × 0.25°) Gridded Rainfall Data Set." *Climate Dynamics* 45, (2015): 755-776. https://doi.org/10.1007/s00382-014-2307-1.

PPPLRC. "Argentina's Climate Risks Map System (SIMARCC)." Accessed February 3, 2020. https://ppp.worldbank.org/public-private-partnership/library/argentina%E2%80%99s-climate-risks-map-system-simarcc.

Razak, A.M.Y. *Industrial Gas Turbines: Performance and Operability*. Amsterdam: Elsevier, 2007.

Romo, Vanessa. "Millions in Texas under Boil-Water Notices Because of Winter Storm." *NPR*, February 17, 2021. https://www.npr.org/sections/live-updates-winter-storms-2021/2021/02/17/968887365/millions-in-texas-under-boil-water-notices-because-of-winter-storm.

Roxy, M.K., Subimal Ghosh, Amey Pathak, R. Athulya, Milind Mujumdar, Raghu Murtugudde, Pascal Terray, and M. Rajaveen. "A Threefold Rise in Widespread Extreme Rain Events Over Central India." *Nature Communications* 8, no. 8 (2017). https://doi.org/10.1038/s41467-017-00744-9.

UN Environment. *Global Environment Outlook – GEO-6: Healthy Planet, Healthy People*. Nairobi: UN Environment, 2019. https://10.1017/9781108627146.

Webster, P.J., and J. Fasullo. "Tropical Meteorology and Climate | Monsoon: Dynamical Theory." In *Encyclopedia of Atmospheric Sciences (Second Edition)*, edited by Gerald R. North, John Pyle, and Fuqing Zhang, 151-164. Cambridge: Academic Press, 2015. https://doi.org/10.1016/B978-0-12-382225-3.00236-X.

Cervigni, Raffaello, Rikard Liden, James E. Neumann, and Kenneth M. Strzepek. *Enhancing the Climate Resilience of Africa's Infrastructure: The Power and Water Sectors*. Washington, DC: World Bank, 2015. https://doi.org/10.1596/978-1-4648-0466-3

CHAPTER 4

Bailis, Robert, Adrian Ghilardi, Omar Masera, and Rudi Drigo. "The Carbon Footprint of Traditional Woodfuels." *Nature*

Climate Change 5, (2015): 266-272. https://doi.org/10.1038/nclimate2491.

Banerjee, Kajori, and Laxmi Kant Dwivedi. "Disparity in Childhood Stunting in India: Relative Importance of Community-Level Nutrition and Sanitary Practices." *PLoS One* 15, no. 9 (2020). https://doi.org/10.1371/journal.pone.0238364.

Bhattacharyya, Subhes C., and Sanusi Ohiare. "The Chinese Electricity Access Model for Rural Electrification." *Energy Policy* 49, (2012): 676-87. https://www.dmu.ac.uk/documents/technology-documents/research-faculties/oasys/project-outputs/peer-reviewed-journal-articles/pj5--chinese-electricity-access---energy-policy-paper.pdf.

Clean Cooking Alliance. "New Report: Lack of Access to Clean Cooking Costs the World $2+ Trillion Annually." Clean Cooking Alliance News, September 24, 2020. Clean Cooking Alliance https://www.cleancookingalliance.org/about/news/09-24-2020-new-report-lack-of-access-to-clean-cooking-costs-the-world-2-trillion-annually.html/, accessed December 20, 2020.

Cohen, Jennie. "Human Ancestors Tamed Fire Earlier Than Thought." *History*, Last modified August 22, 2018. https://www.history.com/news/human-ancestors-tamed-fire-earlier-than-thought.

Ellegård, Anders. "Cooking Fuel Smoke and Respiratory Symptoms among Women in Low-income Areas in Maputo." *Environmental Health Perspectives* 104, no. 9 (September 1996):

980-985. https://ehp.niehs.nih.gov/doi/pdf/10.1289/ehp.104-1469451.

Energy Sector Management Assistance Program (ESMAP), *The State of Access to Modern Energy Cooking Services*. Washington, DC: World Bank. https://openknowledge.worldbank.org/handle/10986/34565.

Epstein, M.B., M.N. Bates, N.K. Arora, K. Balakrishnan, D.W. Jack, and K.R. Smith. "Household Fuels, Low Birth Weight, and Neonatal Death in India: The Separate Impacts of Biomass, Kerosene, and Coal." *International Journal of Hygiene and Environmental Health* 216, no. 5 (August 2013): 523-532. https://doi.org/10.1016/j.ijheh.2012.12.006.

Islam, Samarul, and Sanjay K. Mohanty. "Maternal Exposure to Cooking Smoke and Risk of Low Birth Weight in India." *Science of the Total Environment* 774, (2021). https://doi.org/10.1016/j.scitotenv.2021.145717.

Keino, Susan, Guy Plasqui, Grace Ettyang, and Bart van den Borne. "Determinants of Stunting and Overweight among Young Children and Adolescents in Sub-saharan Africa." *Food and Nutrition Bulletin* 35, no. 2 (2014). https://doi.org/10.1177/156482651403500203.

Lim, Stephen S., Theo Vos, Abraham D Flaxman, Goodarz Danaei, Kenji Shibuya, Heather Adair-Rohani, Mohammad A AlMazroa, Markus Amann, H Ross Anderson, Kathryn G Andrews, Martin Aryee, Charles Atkinson, Loraine J Bacchus, Adil N Bahalim, Kalpana Balakrishnan, John Balmes, Suzanne Barker-Collo, Amanda Baxter, Michelle L Bell, Jed D Blore, Fiona

Blyth, Carissa Bonner, Guilherme Borges, Rupert Bourne, Michel Boussinesq, Michael Brauer, Peter Brooks, Nigel G Bruce, Bert Brunekreef, Claire Bryan-Hancock, Chiara Bucello, Rachelle Buchbinder, Fiona Bull, Richard T Burnett, Tim E Byers, Bianca Calabria, Jonathan Carapetis, Emily Carnahan, Zoe Chafe, Fiona Charlson, Honglei Chen, Jian Shen Chen, Andrew Tai-Ann Cheng, Jennifer Christine Child, Aaron Cohen, K Ellicott Colson, Benjamin C Cowie, Sarah Darby, Susan Darling, Adrian Davis, Louisa Degenhardt, Frank Dentener, Don C Des Jarlais, Karen Devries, Mukesh Dherani, Eric L Ding, E Ray Dorsey, Tim Driscoll, Karen Edmond, Suad Eltahir Ali, Rebecca E Engell, Patricia J Erwin, Saman Fahimi, Gail Falder, Farshad Farzadfar, Alize Ferrari, Mariel M Finucane, Seth Flaxman, Francis Gerry R Fowkes, Greg Freedman, Michael K Freeman, Emmanuela Gakidou, Santu Ghosh, Edward Giovannucci, Gerhard Gmel, Kathryn Graham, Rebecca Grainger, Bridget Grant, David Gunnell, Hialy R Gutierrez, Wayne Hall, Hans W Hoek, Anthony Hogan, H Dean Hosgood III, Damian Hoy, Howard Hu, Bryan J Hubbell, Sally J Hutchings, Sydney E Ibeanusi, Gemma L Jacklyn, Rashmi Jasrasaria, Jost B Jonas, Haidong Kan, John A Kanis, Nicholas Kassebaum, Norito Kawakami, Young-Ho Khang, Shahab Khatibzadeh, Jon-Paul Khoo, Cindy Kok, Francine Laden, Ratilal Lalloo, Qing Lan, Tim Lathlean, Janet L Leasher, James Leigh, Yang Li, John Kent Lin, Steven E Lipshultz, Stephanie London, Rafael Lozano, Yuan Lu, Joelle Mak, Reza Malekzadeh, Leslie Mallinger, Wagner Marcenes, Lyn March, Robin Marks, Randall Martin, Paul McGale, John McGrath, Sumi Mehta, Ziad A Memish, George A Mensah, Tony R Merriman, Renata Micha, Catherine Michaud, Vinod Mishra, Khayriyyah Mohd Hanafi ah, Ali A Mokdad, Lidia Morawska, Dariush Mozaff arian, Tasha Murphy, Mohsen Naghavi, Bruce Neal,

Paul K Nelson, Joan Miquel Nolla, Rosana Norman, Casey Olives, Saad B Omer, Jessica Orchard, Richard Osborne, Bart Ostro, Andrew Page, Kiran D Pandey, Charles D H Parry, Erin Passmore, Jayadeep Patra, Neil Pearce, Pamela M Pelizzari, Max Petzold, Michael R Phillips, Dan Pope, C Arden Pope III, John Powles, Mayuree Rao, Homie Razavi, Eva A Rehfuess, Jürgen T Rehm, Beate Ritz, Frederick P Rivara, Thomas Roberts, Carolyn Robinson, Jose A Rodriguez-Portales, Isabelle Romieu, Robin Room, Lisa C Rosenfeld, Ananya Roy, Lesley Rushton, Joshua A Salomon, Uchechukwu Sampson, Lidia Sanchez-Riera, Ella Sanman, Amir Sapkota, Soraya Seedat, Peilin Shi, Kevin Shield, Rupak Shivakoti, Gitanjali M Singh, David A Sleet, Emma Smith, Kirk R Smith, Nicolas J C Stapelberg, Kyle Steenland, Heidi Stöckl, Lars Jacob Stovner, Kurt Straif, Lahn Straney, George D Thurston, Jimmy H Tran, Rita Van Dingenen, Aaron van Donkelaar, J Lennert Veerman, Lakshmi Vijayakumar, Robert Weintraub, Myrna M Weissman, Richard A White, Harvey Whiteford, Steven T Wiersma, James D Wilkinson, Hywel C Williams, Warwick Williams, Nicholas Wilson, Anthony D Woolf, Paul Yip, Jan M Zielinski, Alan D Lopez, Christopher J L Murray, and Majid Ezzati. "A Comparative Risk Assessment of Burden of Disease and Injury Attributable to 67 Risk Factors and Risk Factor Clusters in 21 Regions, 1990–2010: A Systematic Analysis for the Global Burden of Disease Study 2010." *The Lancet* 380, no. 9859 (2010): 2224-2260. https://doi.org/10.1016/S0140-6736(12)61766-8.

Malla, Sunil, and Govinda R. Timilsina. *Household Cooking Fuel Choice and Adoption of Improved Cookstoves in Developing Countries: A Review.* Policy Research Working Paper;No. 6903. Washington, DC: World Bank, 2014. https://openknowledge.worldbank.org/handle/10986/18775.

Modi, V., S. McDade, D. Lallement, and L. Saghir. *Energy Services for the Millennium Development Goals*. New York: UNDP and The World Bank, 2005.

Mbungu, Grace Kageni. "Lack of Clean Cooking Energy Aggravates Coronavirus Impact in Africa." *Institute for Advanced Sustainability Studies*, June 05, 2020. https://www.iass-potsdam.de/en/blog/2020/05/lack-clean-cooking-energy-aggravates-coronavirus-impact-africa.

Puzzolo, Elisa, H. Zerriffi, E. Carter, H. Clemens, H. Stokes, P. Jagger, J. Rosenthal, and H. Petach. "Growth Faltering Is Associated with Altered Brain Functional Connectivity and Cognitive Outcomes in Urban Bangladeshi Children Exposed to Early Adversity." *BMC Medicine* 17:199, (2019). https://doi.org/10.1029/2019GH000208

Sustainable Energy For All. "Seforall Clean Cooking in Rwanda - Africa (Long Version)." December 18, 2018. Video, 4:29. https://www.youtube.com/watch?v=2kzd4pM2S-Y&t=138s&ab_channel=SustainableEnergyForAll.

Tanigawa, Sarah. "Fact Sheet | Biogas: Converting Waste to Energy." Environmental and Energy Study Institute, Accessed November 28, 2020. https://www.eesi.org/papers/view/fact-sheet-biogasconverting-waste-to-energy.

US Energy Information Administration. "Natural Gas Explained." Accessed January 2, 2020. https://www.eia.gov/energyexplained/natural-gas/.

WHO. "Household Air Pollution and Health." WHO Fact Sheets, Accessed November 3, 2020. https://www.who.int/news-room/fact-sheets/detail/household-air-pollution-and-health.

Xie, Wanze, Sarah K. G. Jensen, Mark Wade, Swapna Kumar, Alissa Westerlund, Shahria H. Kakon, Rashidul Haque, William A. Petri, and Charles A. Nelson. "Supply Considerations for Scaling up Clean Cooking Fuels for Household Energy in Low- and Middle-Income Countries." *GeoHealth* 3, (2019): 370-390. https://doi.org/10.1186/s12916-019-1431-5.

CHAPTER 5

ABC News. "Egyptian Politicians Caught Discussing Plan to Sabotage Ethiopian Dam." *ABC News*, June 4, 2013. https://www.abc.net.au/news/2013-06-05/egyptian-politicians-caught-in-on-air-ethiopia-gaffe/4733544.

Al Jazeera. "Ethiopia's Abiy Ahmed Issues Warning over Renaissance Dam." *Al Jazeera*, October 22, 2019. https://www.aljazeera.com/news/2019/10/22/ethiopias-abiy-ahmed-issues-warning-over-renaissance-dam.

Atkin, Emily. "Climate Change Is Aggravating the Suffering in Yemen." *The New Republic*, November 5, 2018. https://newrepublic.com/article/152011/climate-change-aggravating-suffering-yemen.

Baconi, Tareq. "Testing the Water: How Water Scarcity Could Destabilise the Middle East and North Africa." *European Council on Foreign Relations*, November 13, 2018. https://ecfr.

eu/publication/how_water_scarcity_could_destabilise_the_middle_east_and_north_africa/.

Borger, Julian. "Darfur Conflict Heralds Era of Wars Triggered by Climate Change, Un Report Warns." *The Guardian*, June 23, 2007. https://www.theguardian.com/environment/2007/jun/23/sudan.climatechange.

Carrington, Damian. "How Water Is Helping to End 'the First Climate Change War'." *The Guardian*, December 18, 2019. https://www.theguardian.com/world/2019/dec/18/how-water-is-helping-to-end-the-first-climate-change-war.

Cascão, Ana Elisa. "Resource-Based Conflict in South Sudan and Gambella (Ethiopia): When Water, Land and Oil MIX with Politics." In *State and Societal Challenges in the Horn of Africa*. Lisboa: Centro de Estudos Internacionais, 2013. http://books.openedition.org/cei/295.

Fantini C, Morgan G, Kumar S, Adeoti T, Reese A, Schouten P, Crosskey S & O'Regan N. *Infrastructure and Peacebuilding: The Role of Infrastructure in Building and Sustaining Peace*. Copenhagen: UNOPS, 2020. https://reliefweb.int/sites/reliefweb.int/files/resources/Infrastructure_Peacebuilding_EN_Web.pdf.

Glinski, Stephanie. "The Price of Water: South Sudan's Capital Goes Thirsty as Costs Soar." *Reuters*, September 30, 2017. https://www.reuters.com/article/us-southsudan-water/the-price-of-water-south-sudans-capital-goes-thirsty-as-costs-soar-idUSKCN1C508J.

Hallett, Vick. "Millions of Women Take a Long Walk with a 40-Pound Water Can." *NPR*, July 7, 2016. https://www.npr.org/sections/goatsandsoda/2016/07/07/484793736/millions-of-women-take-a-long-walk-with-a-40-pound-water-can.

Heffez, Adam. "How Yemen Chewed Itself Dry." *Foreign Affairs*, July 23, 2013. https://www.foreignaffairs.com/articles/yemen/2013-07-23/how-yemen-chewed-itself-dry.

Jones, Stephen, and Simon Howarth. *Supporting Infrastructure Development in Fragile and Conflict-Affected States: Learning from Experience*. Oxford: Oxford Policy Management, 2012. https://gsdrc.org/document-library/supporting-infrastructure-development-in-fragile-and-conflict-affected-states-learning-from-experience/.

Kochhar, Kalpana, Catherine Pattillo, Yan Sun, Nujin Suphaphiphat, Andrew Swiston, Robert Tchaidze, Benedict Clements, Stefania Fabrizio, Valentina Flamini, Laure Redifer, Harald Finger, and an IMF Staff Team. *Is the Glass Half Empty or Half Full? Issues in Managing Water Challenges and Policy Instruments*. Washington, DC: IMF, 2015. https://www.imf.org/en/Publications/Staff-Discussion-Notes/Issues/2016/12/31/Is-the-Glass-Half-Empty-Or-Half-Full-Issues-in-Managing-Water-Challenges-and-Policy-42938.

Lazarou, Elena. *Water in the Israeli-Palestinian Conflict*. Brussels: European Parliamentary Research Service, 2016. https://www.europarl.europa.eu/RegData/etudes/BRIE/2016/573916/EPRS_BRI%282016%29573916_EN.pdf.

OECD. *States of Fragility 2018*. Paris: OECD Publishing, 2018. https://doi.org/10.1787/fa5a6770-en.

OECD. *States of Fragility 2020*. Paris: OECD Publishing, 2020. https://doi.org/10.1787/ba7c22e7-en.

Raphelson, Samantha. "In Africa, War over Water Looms as Ethiopia Nears Completion of Nile River Dam." *NPR*, February 27, 2018. https://www.npr.org/2018/02/27/589240174/in-africa-war-over-water-looms-as-ethiopia-nears-completion-of-nile-river-dam?t=1595668819363.

Reuters. "Study Estimates 190,000 People Killed in South Sudan's Civil War." *Reuters*, September 26, 2018. https://www.reuters.com/article/us-southsudan-unrest-toll/study-estimates-190000-people-killed-in-south-sudans-civil-war-idUSKCN-1M626R.

Sova, Chase. "The First Climate Change Conflict." *Blog & News. World Food Program USA*, November 30, 2017. https://www.wfpusa.org/articles/the-first-climate-change-conflict/.

Trew, Bel. "South Sudan, Where a Water Crisis Is Leading to Child Kidnappings and Rape." *Independent*, May 31, 2019. https://www.independent.co.uk/news/world/africa/south-sudan-water-crisis-war-conflict-women-a8853176.html.

United Nations Security Council. "Final Report of the Group of Experts on the Democratic Republic of Congo Submitted in Accordance with Paragraph 5 of Security Council Resolution 1952 (2010), S/2011/738." United Nations, December 2, 2011. https://www.undocs.org/S/2011/738

United Nations; World Bank. *Pathways for Peace: Inclusive Approaches to Preventing Violent Conflict*. Washington, DC: World Bank, 2018. https://openknowledge.worldbank.org/handle/10986/28337.

UNOPS. "World Bank and UNOPS Sign Solar Project to Restore Electricity to over One Million Yemenis." UNOPS, April 27, 2018. UNOPS website. https://www.unops.org/news-and-stories/news/world-bank-and-unops-sign-solar-project-to-restore-electricity-to-over-one-million-yemenis.

USAID. "South Sudan: Water." Where We Work. Last modified January 21, 2021. https://www.usaid.gov/africa/south-sudan/water.

USAID. "PRT Quick Impact Projects." Last modified May 07, 2019. https://www.usaid.gov/node/51861.

Whitehead, Frederika. "Water Scarcity in Yemen: The Country's Forgotten Conflict." *The Guardian*, April 2, 2015. https://www.theguardian.com/global-development-professionals-network/2015/apr/02/water-scarcity-yemen-conflict.

Varisco, Daniel. "Pumping Yemen Dry: A History of Yemen's Water Crisis." *Human Ecology* 47, (2019): 317-329. https://doi.org/10.1007/s10745-019-0070-y.

Ward, Mark. "Quick Impact Projects Slow Progress in Afghanistan." *Boston Globe*, October 15, 2009. http://archive.boston.com/bostonglobe/editorial_opinion/oped/articles/2009/10/15/quick_impact_projects_slow_progress_in_afghanistan/.

Wee, Asbjorn, Julia Lendorfer, Jaimie Bleck, and Charlotte Yaiche. *State Legitimacy, Stability and Social Cohesion in Low Population Density Areas: The Case of Northern Mali*. Berkely: University of California Berkeley, 2014. https://cega.berkeley.edu/assets/miscellaneous_files/130_-_Wee_-_Mali_-_Governance_and_service_delivery_in_low_density_-_ABCA_submission.pdf.

World Bank. *Beyond Scarcity: Water Security in the Middle East and North Africa*. MENA Development Series. Washington, DC: World Bank, 2017. https://openknowledge.worldbank.org/handle/10986/27659.

World Bank. "Fragility and Conflict: On the Front Lines of the Fight against Poverty." *World Bank*, February 27, 2020. https://www.worldbank.org/en/topic/poverty/publication/fragility-conflict-on-the-front-lines-fight-against-poverty.

World Bank. "Fragility, Conflict, & Violence Overview." *World Bank*, accessed December 19, 2020. https://www.worldbank.org/en/topic/fragilityconflictviolence/overview#:~:text=Fragility%2C%20conflict%2C%20and%20violence%20(,80%25%20of%20all%20humanitarian%20needs.

World Bank. "Future Impact of Climate Change Visible Now in Yemen." *World Bank*, November 24, 2014. https://www.worldbank.org/en/news/feature/2014/11/24/future-impact-of-climate-change-visible-now-in-yemen.

World Bank. *Republic of Yemen: Unlocking the Potential for Economic Growth*. Washington, DC: World Bank, 2015. https://openknowledge.worldbank.org/handle/10986/23660.

World Economic Forum. *Global Risks 2015: 10th Edition*. Cologny: World Economic Forum, 2015. http://www3.weforum.org/docs/WEF_Global_Risks_2015_Report15.pdf.

CHAPTER 6

Aigner, John. "The Logic behind the Bonds That Eat Your Money." *Bloomberg*, July 24, 2019. https://www.bloomberg.com/graphics/2019-negative-yield-debt/.

Bhattacharya, Amar, Mattia Romani, and Nicholas Stern. *Infrastructure for Development: Meeting the Challenge*. CCCEP, LSE, G24, 2012. https://www.lse.ac.uk/GranthamInstitute/wp-content/uploads/2014/03/PP-infrastructure-for-development-meeting-the-challenge.pdf

Congressional Research Service. *Multilateral Development Banks: Overview and Issues for Congress*. Washington, DC: Congressional Research Service, 2020. https://fas.org/sgp/crs/row/R41170.pdf

CPP Investment Board. "Canada Pension Plan Investment Board to Invest in Cipali Toll Road in Indonesia." California Public Pension Investment Board press release, September 19, 2019. https://cdn4.cppinvestments.com/wp-content/uploads/migrated/documents/2101/cppib-cipali-toll-road-press-relelase-sept-19-2019-EN_NFB6oQV.pdf.

Fay, Marianne, Hyoung Il Lee, Massimo Mastruzzi, Sungmin Han, Moonkyoung Cho. *Hitting the Trillion Mark: A Look at How Much Countries Are Spending on Infrastructure*. Policy Research Working Paper, No. 8730. Washington, DC: World

Bank, 2019. https://openknowledge.worldbank.org/handle/10986/31234

Green, Jeffrey M. "What Is a Financial Instrument?" *The Balance*, Last Modified January 11, 2021. https://www.thebalance.com/what-is-a-financial-instrument-5095041.

Hamadeh, Nada, Mizuki Yamanaka, and Edie Purdie. "The Size of the World Economy in 2019: A Baseline from Which to Measure the Impact of COVID-19 and Track Economic Recovery." *Data Blog*. World Bank, July 28, 2020. https://blogs.worldbank.org/opendata/size-world-economy-2019-baseline-which-measure-impact-covid-19-and-track-economic-recovery.

Inderst, Georg, and Fiona Stewart. *Institutional Investment in Infrastructure in Emerging Markets and Developing Economies*. Washington, DC: Public-Private Infrastructure Advisory Facility (PPIAF), 2014. https://mpra.ub.uni-muenchen.de/62522/1/MPRA_paper_62522.pdf.

Kenny, Thomas. "The Safety of US Treasuries and Government Bonds." *The Balance*, Last Modified October 21, 2019. https://www.thebalance.com/how-safe-are-u-s-treasuries-417129.

Mohamed, Theron. "The Entire Us Yield Curve Plunged below 1% for the First Time Ever. Here's Why That's a Big Red Flag for Investors." *Insider*, March 9, 2020. https://markets.businessinsider.com/news/stocks/us-treasury-yield-curve-below-1-percent-red-flag-investors-2020-3-1028975968.

Mullen, Cormac, and John Aigner. "World's Negative-Yielding Debt Pile Hits $18 Trillion Record." *Bloomberg*, December 10,

2020. https://www.bloomberg.com/news/articles/2020-12-11/world-s-negative-yield-debt-pile-at-18-trillion-for-first-time#:~:text=The%20market%20value%20of%20the,for%20the%20first%20time%20Friday.

Sachs, Jeffrey. *Common Wealth: Economics for a Crowded Planet*. London: Penguin Books, 2008.

SIFMA. *2020 Capital Markets Fact Book*. New York: SIFMA, 2020. https://www.sifma.org/wp-content/uploads/2020/09/US-Fact-Book-2020-SIFMA.pdf.

Tennessee Valley Authority (TVA). "About TVA." Accessed October 17, 2020. https://www.tva.com/about-tva.

UNOPS. "World Bank and UNOPS Sign Solar Project to Restore Electricity to over One Million Yemenis." UNOPS, April 27, 2018. UNOPS website. https://www.unops.org/news-and-stories/news/world-bank-and-unops-sign-solar-project-to-restore-electricity-to-over-one-million-yemenis.

US Energy Information Administration. "Investor-Owned Utilities Served 72% of US Electricity Customers in 2017." Today in Energy. Last modified August 15, 2019. https://www.eia.gov/todayinenergy/detail.php?id=40913.

United Nations, Inter-agency Task Force on Financing for Development. *Financing for Sustainable Development Report 2019*. New York: United Nations, 2019. https://developmentfinance.un.org/fsdr2019.

World Bank. *Supporting Countries in Unprecedented Times: Annual Report 2020.* Washington, DC: World Bank, 2020. https://www.worldbank.org/en/about/annual-report#anchor-annual.

Kim, Jim Yong. "Doesn't Everyone Deserve a Chance at a Good Life?" Filmed April 2017 in New York, NY. TED video, 22:03. https://www.ted.com/talks/jim_yong_kim_doesn_t_everyone_deserve_a_chance_at_a_good_life?language=en.

CHAPTER 7

Ang, Andrew. *Asset Management: A Systematic Approach to Factor Investing.* Oxford: Oxford University Press, 2014.

Bagínski, Paweł. "Infrastructure as an Asset Class." *Central European Financial Observer,* August 23, 2019. https://www.obserwatorfinansowy.pl/in-english/business/infrastructure-as-an-asset-class/#:~:text=One%20indication%20of%20source%20of,investors%2C%20in%20particular%20pension%20funds.&text=Due%20to%20their%20long%2Dterm,to%20make%20long%2Dterm%20investments.

Blanc-Brude, Frédéric, Tim Whittaker, and Jing-Li Yim. *Investor Perceptions of Infrastructure, 2017: From Investment Plans to Price Discovery.* Singapore: EDEHC Infrastructure Institute, 2017. https://cdn.gihub.org/umbraco/media/1820/gih-edhec-investor-survey-2017-web.pdf.

Center for Global Development. "Is There Any Hope for Mobilizing the Trillions Needed for the SDGs" *Debates in Development. Center for Global Development,* accessed February 3, 2021. https://www.cgdev.org/debate/hope-for-funding-SDGs.

Kumar, Sanjiv, Neeta Kumar, and Saxena Vivekadhish. "Millennium Development Goals (MDGs) to Sustainable Development Goals (SDGs): Addressing Unfinished Agenda and Strengthening Sustainable Development and Partnership." *Indian Journal of Community Medicine* 41, no.1 (2016): 1-4. https://doi.org/10.4103/0970-0218.170955.

McMichael, Phillip. *Development and Social Change, 6th Edition.* Thousand Oaks: Sage Publications, 2016.

Inderst, Georg, and Fiona Stewart. *Institutional Investment in Infrastructure in Emerging Markets and Developing Economies.* Washington, DC: Public-Private Infrastructure Advisory Facility (PPIAF), 2014. https://mpra.ub.uni-muenchen.de/62522/1/MPRA_paper_62522.pdf.

OECD/The World Bank/UN Environment, *Financing Climate Futures.* Paris: OECD Publishing, 2018. https://doi.org/10.1787/9789264308114-en.

OECD. *Green Infrastructure in the Decade for Delivery: Assessing Institutional Investment.* Paris: OECD Publishing, 2020. https://doi.org/10.1787/24090344.

OECD. "OECD and Donor Countries Working to Focus Development Efforts on COVID-19 Crisis, Building on a Rise in Official Aid in 2019." OECD press release, April 16, 2020. OECD website. https://www.oecd.org/development/oecd-and-donor-countries-working-to-focus-development-efforts-on-covid-19-crisis-building-on-a-rise-in-official-aid-in-2019.htm.

Preqin. *2020 Preqin Global Infrastructure Report*. London: Preqin, 2020. https://docs.preqin.com/samples/2020-Preqin-Global-Infrastructure-Report-Sample-Pages.pdf.

PwC/GIIA. *Global Infrastructure Investment: The Role of Private Capital in the Delivery of Essential Assets and Services*. London: PricewaterhouseCooper and Global Infrastructure Investor Association, 2017. https://www.pwc.com/gx/en/industries/assets/pwc-giia-global-infrastructure-investment-2017-web.pdf.

Sachs, Jeffrey. *Common Wealth: Economics for a Crowded Planet*. London: Penguin Books, 2008.

Sharma, Rajiv. "Infrastructure: An Emerging Asset Class for Institutional Investors." Working Paper, Stanford University Global Projects Center, 2016. https://gpc.stanford.edu/sites/g/files/sbiybj8226/f/infrastructure-emergingassetclassworkingpaper.pdf

Schwartz, Jordan. "Institutional Investment in Infrastructure: A View from the Bridge of a Development Agency." *Private Sector Development Blog. World Bank*, April 16, 2015. https://blogs.worldbank.org/psd/institutional-investment-infrastructure-view-bridge-development-agency.

SWFI. "Top 100 Largest Public Pension Rankings by Total Assets." Accessed January 20, 2021. https://www.swfinstitute.org/fund-rankings/public-pension.

SWFI. "Top 95 Largest Sovereign Wealth Fund Rankings by Total Assets." Accessed January 20, 2021. https://www.swfinstitute.org/fund-rankings/public-pension.

top100funds. "California Public Employees Retirement System (Calpers)." Accessed January 20, 2021. https://www.top1000funds.com/asset_owner/california-public-employees-retirement-system-calpers/#:~:text=The%20California%20Public%20Employees'%20Retirement,%2C%20retirees%2C%20and%20their%20families.

Woetzel, Jonathan, Nicklas Garemo, Jan Mischke, and Brendan Halleman. *Bridging Global Infrastructure Gaps.* McKinsey Global Institute, 2018. https://www.mckinsey.com/business-functions/operations/our-insights/bridging-global-infrastructure-gaps.

World Bank. *From Billions to Trillions: MDB Contributions to Financing for Development.* Washington, DC: World Bank, 2015. https://doi.org/10.1787/24090344. http://documents1.worldbank.org/curated/en/602761467999349576/pdf/98023-BR-SecM2015-0233-IDA-SecM2015-0147-IFC-SecM2015-0105-MIGA-SecM2015-0061-Box391499B-OUO-9.pdf.

CHAPTER 8

Bhattacharya, Amar, Joshua P. Meltzer, Jeremy Oppenheim, and Nicholas Stern. *Delivering on Sustainable Infrastructure for Better Development and Better Climate.* Washington DC: Brookings Institution, 2016. https://www.brookings.edu/wp-content/uploads/2016/12/global_122316_delivering-on-sustainable-infrastructure.pdf.

Bielenberg, Aaron, Mike Kerlin, Jeremy Oppenheim, and Melissa Roberts. *Financing Change: How to Mobilize Private Sector Financing for Sustainable Infrastructure.* McKinsey Center for

Business and Environment, 2016. https://newclimateeconomy.report/workingpapers/wp-content/uploads/sites/5/2016/04/Financing_change_How_to_mobilize_private-sector_financing_for_sustainable-_infrastructure.pdf.

Cavallo, Eduardo, Andrew Powell, and Tomás Serebrisky, eds. *From Structures to Services: The Path to Better Infrastructure in Latin America and the Caribbean*. Washington, DC: Inter-American Development Bank, 2020. https://doi.org/10.18235/0002506

G20 Development Working Group. *Report on Infrastructure Agenda and Response to the Assessments of Project Preparation Facilities in Asia and Africa*. Cancún: G20, accessed December 20, 2020. https://www.tralac.org/images/docs/6283/g20-dwg-report-on-infrastructure-agenda-and-response-to-the-assessments-of-project-preparation-facilities.pdf.

Inderst, Georg, and Fiona Stewart. *Institutional Investment in Infrastructure in Emerging Markets and Developing Economies*. Washington, DC: Public-Private Infrastructure Advisory Facility (PPIAF), 2014. https://mpra.ub.uni-muenchen.de/62522/1/MPRA_paper_62522.pdf.

Kline, Sarah. "Answering the Infrastructure Finance FAQs." *Bipartisan Policy Center*, January 06, 2017. https://bipartisanpolicy.org/blog/infrastructure-finance-faqs/#:~:text=Financing%20allows%20projects%20to%20be,is%20needed%20to%20repay%20financing.

O'DEA, "Emerging Markets: Just Too Risky to Bear?" *IPE Real Assets*, June 2015. https://realassets.ipe.com/infrastructure/emerging-markets-just-too-risky-to-bear/10008523.article.

OECD. *Green Infrastructure in the Decade for Delivery: Assessing Institutional Investment*. Paris: OECD Publishing, 2020. https://doi.org/10.1787/24090344.

Phibbs, Peter. "Driving Alone: Sydney's Cross City Tunnel." *Built Environment* 34, no. 3 (2008): 364-374. http://www.jstor.org/stable/23289790

PwC/GIIA. *Global Infrastructure Investment: The Role of Private Capital in the Delivery of Essential Assets and Services*. London: PricewaterhouseCooper and Global Infrastructure Investor Association, 2017. https://www.pwc.com/gx/en/industries/assets/pwc-giia-global-infrastructure-investment-2017-web.pdf.

Runde, Daniel, Helen Moser, and Erin Nealer. *Barriers to Bankable Infrastructure: Incentivizing Private Investment to Fill the Global Infrastructure Gap*. Washington, DC: Center for Strategic and International Studies, 2016. https://csis-website-prod.s3.amazonaws.com/s3fs-public/publication/160308_Moser_BarriersBankableInfrastructure_Web.pdf.

Sharma, Rajiv. "Infrastructure: An Emerging Asset Class for Institutional Investors." Working Paper, Stanford University Global Projects Center, 2016. https://gpc.stanford.edu/sites/g/files/sbiybj8226/f/infrastructure-emergingassetclassworkingpaper.pdf

CHAPTER 9

Bhattacharya, Amar, Joshua P. Meltzer, Jeremy Oppenheim, and Nicholas Stern. *Delivering on Sustainable Infrastructure for Better Development and Better Climate*. Washington DC:

Brookings Institution, 2016. https://www.brookings.edu/wp-content/uploads/2016/12/global_122316_delivering-on-sustainable-infrastructure.pdf.

Egypt Today. "Benban Solar Project Biggest in the World: Min." *Egypt Today*, July 03, 2018. https://www.egypttoday.com/Article/1/53289/Benban-Solar-Project-biggest-in-the-world-Min.

ESMAP. *Maximizing Finance for Development in Egypt's Energy Sector*. Washington, DC: World Bank, 2019. http://documents1.worldbank.org/curated/en/780061567532224696/pdf/Maximizing-Finance-for-Development-in-Egypts-Energy-Sector.pdf.

Center for Energy Finance, "Offtake risk: The Buck Stops Here." *CEEW*, July 16, 2019, accessed March 3, 2021. https://cef.ceew.in/masterclass/analysis/offtake-risk-the-buck-stops-here.

Coady, David, Ian Parry, Louis Sears, and Baoping Shang. "How Large are Global Energy Subsidies." IMF Working Paper, International Monetary Fund, 2015. https://www.imf.org/external/pubs/ft/wp/2015/wp15105.pdf.

Kingsley, Patrick. "Egypt Suffers Regular Blackouts Due to Worst Energy Crisis in Decades." *The Guardian*, August 20, 2014. https://www.theguardian.com/world/2014/aug/20/egypt-blackouts-energy-crisis-power-cuts.

Milken Institute. "Filling the Global Infrastructure Gap." August 26, 2019. Video, 57:27. https://www.youtube.com/watch?v=VqlJoLX2qvg&t=2s&ab_channel=MilkenInstitute.

Scheier, Rachel. "The World's Largest Solar Farm Rises in the Remote Egyptian Desert" *Los Angeles Times,* July 30, 2018. https://www.latimes.com/world/middleeast/la-fg-egypt-green-power-20180730-story.html.

Schwartztein, Peter. "Can Egypt's Crisis Help Clean Energy Gain Traction?" *National Geographic,* October 2, 2014. https://www.nationalgeographic.com/science/article/141003-egypt-renewable-energy.

World Bank. "Cash Transfers: Empowering Egyptian Women to Achieve Their Goals." *World Bank*, March 14, 2019. https://www.worldbank.org/en/news/feature/2019/03/14/egypt-empowering-women-trough-cash-transfers.

CHAPTER 10

Bhattacharya, Amar, Joshua P. Meltzer, Jeremy Oppenheim, and Nicholas Stern. *Delivering on Sustainable Infrastructure for Better Development and Better Climate.* Washington DC: Brookings Institution, 2016. https://www.brookings.edu/wp-content/uploads/2016/12/global_122316_delivering-on-sustainable-infrastructure.pdf.

Eberhard, Anton, Joel Kolker, and James Leigland. *South Africa's Renewable Energy IPP Procurement Program: Success Factors and Lessons.* Washington, DC: Public-Private Infrastructure Advisory Facility (PPIAF), 2014. http://www.gsb.uct.ac.za/files/PPIAFReport.pdf.

Gibbons, John. "Zambians Brace for Water Shortage despite Recent Rainfall." *The Guardian,* March 12, 2020. https://www.

theguardian.com/world/2020/mar/12/zambians-water-shortage-drought-lake-rainfall#:~:text=Zambia%20is%20facing%20severe%20water,worryingly%20low%20despite%20recent%20rains.&text=When%20running%20at%20capacity%2C%20the,than%202.1GW%20of%20electricity.

Haria, Shivani, and Imaduddin Ahmed. "Increasing Tariffs to Prevent Another Electricity Crisis in Zambia." *International Growth Centre*, March 30, 2020. https://www.theigc.org/blog/increasing-tariffs-to-prevent-another-electricity-crisis-in-zambia/.

Hussain, Ali Abid, Selim Jeddi, Kannan Lakmeeharan, and Hasan Muzaffar. "Unlocking Private-Sector Financing in Emerging-Markets Infrastructure." *McKinsey & Company*, October 10, 2019. https://www.mckinsey.com/industries/private-equity-and-principal-investors/our-insights/unlocking-private-sector-financing-in-emerging-markets-infrastructure.

IFC. "Scaling Solar Delivers Low-Cost Clean Energy for Zambia." International Finance Corporation news release, June 2016. IFC website. https://www.ifc.org/wps/wcm/connect/news_ext_content/ifc_external_corporate_site/news+and+events/news/scaling+solar+delivers+low+cost+clean+energy+for+zambia, accessed January 13, 2021.

IFC. "Unlocking Low-Cost, Large-Scale Solar Power." International Finance Corporation news release, May 2016. IFC website. https://www.ifc.org/wps/wcm/connect/news_ext_content/ifc_external_corporate_site/news+and+events/news/scaling+solar+unlocking+low+cost+large+scale+solar+power, accessed January 13, 2021.

Inderst, Georg. "Financing Development: Private Capital Mobilization and Institutional Investors." Discussion Paper, Inderst Advisory, 2021. https://papers.ssrn.com/sol3/papers.cfm?abstract_id=3806742

Johnson, Marty. "Zambia Warns Climate Change Has LED to Worst Drought in a Century." *The Hill*, December 06, 2019. https://thehill.com/policy/energy-environment/473413-zambia-warns-climate-change-has-led-to-worst-drought-in-a-century.

KPMG. *Global Infrastructure: Asset Recycling and Infra Capital.* KPMG, 2020. https://assets.kpmg/content/dam/kpmg/sg/pdf/2020/07/Global-infrastructure-asset-recycling-and-infra-capital.pdf.

Marsh & McLennan Companies. *Infrastructure Asset Recycling: Insights for Governments and Investors.* Marsh & McLennan Companies, Asia Pacific Risk Center, 2018. https://www.marsh.com/th/en/insights/research/infrastructure-asset-recycling-insights-for-governments-and-investors.html#:~:text=Infrastructure%20asset%20recycling%20involves%20the,being%20reinvested%20in%20new%20infrastructure.

OECD. *Green Infrastructure in the Decade for Delivery: Assessing Institutional Investment.* Paris: OECD Publishing, 2020. https://doi.org/10.1787/24090344.

OECD. *Breaking Silos: Actions to Develop Infrastructure as an Asset Class and Address the Information Gap.* Paris: OECD Publishing, 2017. http://www.oecd.org/daf/fin/private-pensions/

Breaking-Silos%20-Actions-to%20Develop-Infrastructure-as-an-Asset-Class-and-Address-the-Information-Gap.pdf.

Phiri, Chris. "Load-Shedding Threatens Water Supply." *Zambia Reports*, September 08, 2015. https://zambiareports.com/2015/09/08/load-shedding-threatens-water-supply/.

Ranjan, Rakesh. "Japan's Univergy to Invest $200 Million in Zambian Solar Projects." *Mercom India*, November 07, 2019. https://mercomindia.com/japan-univergy-invest-zambian-solar-projects/.

Rio, Pablo del. *Auctions for Renewable Support in Zambia: Instruments and Lessons Learnt*. AURES, 2020. https://www.auresproject.eu/sites/auresproject.eu/files/media/documents/zambia_final.pdf.

Solar Aid. "The Zambia Drought." *Solar Aid*, November 07, 2019. https://solar-aid.org/news/the-zambia-drought-the-different-faces-of-climate-change-part-2/.

US PREF. *Renewable Energy Finance Fundamentals*. Washington, DC: American Council on Renewable Energy, accessed February 23, 2021. https://silo.tips/download/renewable-energy-finance-fundamentals.

World Bank. "Unlocking Low-Cost, Large-Scale Solar Power in Zambia." *World Bank*, May 14, 2019. https://www.worldbank.org/en/news/feature/2019/05/14/unlocking-low-cost-large-scale-solar-power-in-zambia.

CHAPTER 11

Abi-Habib, Maria. "Millions Had Risen Out of Poverty. Coronavirus Is Pulling Them Back." *New York Times*, April 30, 2020. https://www.nytimes.com/2020/04/30/world/asia/coronavirus-poverty-unemployment.html.

Bailey, Ronald. "Is 'King Solar' Now the Cheapest Electricity Source Ever?" *Reason*, October 28, 2020. https://reason.com/2020/10/28/is-king-solar-now-the-cheapest-electricity-source-ever/.

Cassim, Ziyad, Borko Handjiski, Jörg Schubert, and Yassir Zouaoui. *The $10 Trillion Rescue: How Governments Can Deliver Impact*. McKinsey & Company, 2020. https://www.mckinsey.com/~/media/McKinsey/Industries/Public%20Sector/Our%20Insights/The%2010%20trillion%20dollar%20rescue%20How%20governments%20can%20deliver%20impact/The-10-trillion-dollar-rescue-How-governments-can-deliver-impact-vF.pdf.

Chilkoti, Avantika, and Gabriele Steinhauser. "COVID's Next Economic Crisis: Developing-Nation Debt." *Wall Street Journal*, July 26, 2020. https://www.wsj.com/articles/covid-coronavirus-developing-nation-africa-debt-crisis-11595455147.

Fink, Larry. "Larry Fink's 2021 Letter to Ceos." *Investor Relations. Black Rock*, January 23, 2021. https://www.blackrock.com/corporate/investor-relations/larry-fink-ceo-letter.

Greenwood, Larry. "COVID-19 and Asia's Infrastructure Imperative." *Center for Strategic & International Studies*, October 06,

2020. https://www.csis.org/analysis/covid-19-and-asias-infrastructure-imperative.

Hua, Jingdong. "The OMFIF/KPMG Series: Sustainable Infrastructure and the Green Transition." Interview by Kat Usita. *The OMFIF Podcast*, OMFIF, July 23, 2020. Audio, 44:09. https://www.omfif.org/podcast/the-omfif-kpmg-series-sustainable-infrastructure-and-the-green-transition/.

International Energy Agency. *World Energy Outlook 2020*. Paris: IEA, 2020. https://www.iea.org/reports/world-energy-outlook-2020/outlook-for-electricity.

IMF. *World Economic Outlook, October 2020: A Long and Difficult Ascent*. Washington, DC: IMF, 2020. https://www.imf.org/en/Publications/WEO/Issues/2020/09/30/world-economic-outlook-october-2020.

Inman, Phillip. "Global Investors Clamour for Safe Haven in UK Government Bonds." *The Guardian*, April 07, 2020. https://www.theguardian.com/business/2020/apr/07/investors-clamour-for-safe-haven-in-uk-government-bonds.

Law, Tara. "2 Million People Have Died from COVID-19 Worldwide." *Time*, January 15, 2021. https://time.com/5930111/2-million-covid-19-deaths/.

Lowenstein, Roger. "Economic History Repeating." *Wall Street Journal*, January 13, 2015. https://www.wsj.com/articles/book-review-hall-of-mirrors-by-barry-eichengreen-1421192283.

PwC. *Cornering the Globe: Capturing Profit Around the World*. London: PricewaterhouseCooper, 2017. https://www.pwc.com/us/en/technology/publications/assets/cornering-the-globe-seeing-green.pdf.

Roosevelt, Franklin Delano. " Acceptance Speech to the 1932 Democratic Convention." Speech, Chicago, July 2, 1932. FDR Library. https://www.fdrlibrary.org/dnc-curriculum-hub.

Shalal, Andrea, and David Lawder. "IMF Chief Economist Says 100 Countries Seek Pandemic Aid; More Resources May Be Needed." *Reuters*, April 14, 2020. https://www.reuters.com/article/us-imf-world-bank-imf-resources/imf-chief-economist-says-100-countries-seek-pandemic-aid-more-resources-may-be-needed-idUSKCN21W2UQ.

Smith, Robert, and Jacob Goldstein. "Where Do We Get $2,000,000,000,000?" March 26, 2020. In *Planet Money*. Podcast, MP3 audio, 20:26. https://www.npr.org/2020/03/26/821787090/episode-985-where-do-we-get-2-000-000-000-000.

Strayed, Cheryl. *American-Made: The Enduring Legacy of the WPA when FDR Put the Nation to Work*. New York: Penguin Random House, 2008.

UN/DESA. *Policy Brief #72: COVID-19 and Sovereign Debt*. New York: UN/DESA, 2020. https://www.un.org/development/desa/dpad/publication/un-desa-policy-brief-72-covid-19-and-sovereign-debt/.

University of Washington. "The Great Depression in Washington State: Economics and Poverty." Accessed January 1, 2021. http://depts.washington.edu/depress/economics_poverty.shtml.

World Bank. *International Debt Statistics 2021*. Washington, DC: World Bank, 2021. https://doi.org/10.1596/978-1-4648-1610-9.

CHAPTER 12

Harvey, Charlotte Bruce. "The Healer." *Brown Alumni Magazine*, February 27, 2007. https://www.brownalumnimagazine.com/articles/2007-02-27/the-healer.

Kim, Jim Yong. "Doesn't Everyone Deserve a Chance at a Good Life?" Filmed April 2017 in New York, NY. TED video, 22:03. https://www.ted.com/talks/jim_yong_kim_doesn_t_everyone_deserve_a_chance_at_a_good_life?language=en.

Kim, Jim Yong. "Jim Yong Kim on Revolutionizing How We Treat the World's Poor." Interview by Ezra Klein. *The OMFIF Podcast*, VOX, March 8, 2016. Audio.

World Bank. "Jim Yong Kim." Accessed February 20, 2021. https://blogs.worldbank.org/team/jim-yong-kim

www.ingramcontent.com/pod-product-compliance
Lightning Source LLC
LaVergne TN
LVHW011808060526
838200LV00053B/3699